Di van Niekerk's

Roses

in silk and organza ribbon

Di van Niekerk's

Roses

in silk and organza ribbon

SEARCH PRESS

For Wilsia Metz –
a rose without thorns

*First published in paperback
in Great Britain 2012
Search Press Limited
Wellwood, North Farm Road,
Tunbridge Wells, Kent, TN2 3DR*

*First published in hardback
in Great Britain 2011*

*Originally published in South Africa in
2011 by Metz Press, 1 Cameronians Ave,
Welgemoed 7530, South Africa*

ISBN 978-1-84448-874-2

*Copyright © Metz Press 2012
Text copyright © Di van Niekerk
Photographs and illustrations copyright
© Di van Niekerk, Metz Press*

Publisher   *Wilsia Metz*
Design and layout   *Liezl Maree*
Proofreader   *Francie Botes*
Illustrations   *Wendy Brittnell*
Photographer   *Ivan Naudé*
Reproduction   *Color/Fuzion*
Printed and bound by WKT Co Ltd, China

Contents

... CONTENTS: THE CHAPTERS

Anatomy of a rose

Corolla or petals

Calyx
- Sepal
- Tube

Stem (peduncle)

Prickles

Petiole

Auricle

Terminal leaf

Leaf

Stipule

Petiole: *The stalk of the leaf.*

Stipule: *A supplementary leaf on the petiole where it meets the stem.*

Auricle: *The ear-like protuberance found at the tip of the stipule.*

Rose hip: *The fruit of the rose which holds the seeds.*

Peduncle: *The main stem of the rose.*

Calyx: *Parts of a flower which grow from the stem (peduncle), primarily the green, leaf-like sepals.*

Sepal: *Part of the calyx. On a rosebud, the green sepals open up to reveal the rose petals. A rose usually has five sepals.*

Did you know?
Roses have prickles, not 'thorns'.

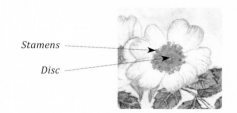

Stamens

Disc

Introduction

Delicate and beautiful, the rose has been a symbol of love since ancient times, and if you love roses, then this is just the book for you.

Learn how to make beautiful, delicate, realistic silk roses and organza leaves ... and have fun making them for a friend or for a special project. Perfect for silk ribbon fans, crazy quilters, fibre artists, card makers, dress designers ... there is a rose in this book for every occasion.

Make a rose and add it to a felted hat or knitted bag or crochet scarf or beaded necklace, or make a lid for a jewellery box ... or make a beautiful rose for that most special outfit of all – your wedding dress.

In this book you will learn brand-new techniques; some easy and some more complex. Whether you learn on the exquisite rose sampler designed for this book, or whether you make only one rose, this is a book that you will refer to often in years to come, especially when you need to make something exceptional.

In this book you will learn more than sixty techniques, many of them brand-new. You will learn how to make sixteen different roses which bloom amongst the latticework of rosebuds, leaves and stems; learn how to make rose petals and rose hips, sepals, stems and leaves, spent roses and stamens, and gorgeous little birds, a bird's nest, and beautiful butterflies, bows and Wisteria ... there is something here for every crafter eager to learn how to create with silk and organza ribbon.

Enjoy yourself!

Love

Di van Niekerk

The rose speaks of love silently, in a language known only to the heart. By Unknown

Getting Started

Transferring designs

Embroidering on a picture has many advantages. It's easy to be creative: there is no need to fill in the entire design – the painted background supports your work as the composition is already in place. It is almost impossible to go wrong! There are several ways to transfer a design onto fabric – choose the method that suits you best.

Enlarging the design

For all the methods discussed, you will need to have the design on page 160 enlarged by 156% to the final size of 29.03 x 38.2cm (11.43 x 15.039"). Use the original design on page 160 for this purpose. Alternatively you could order the printed rose sampler from your nearest stockist. Visit our website www.dicraft.co.za and search for: stockists worldwide, or order it directly from my website by searching for the rose sampler printed panel.

USING HEAT TRANSFERS

New advances in technology allow you to easily transfer coloured designs onto fabric. Transfer paper is probably the best choice for putting images onto fabric. It is a quick, easy, clean, colourfast method and it really works!

The method is quite simple:
1. The original design is copied onto transfer paper.
2. The paper is placed face down onto the fabric
3. Heat is used to seal the design onto the fabric.
4. The transfer backing is peeled off, leaving the design on the fabric. For this method, you have the following choices: you can purchase transfer sheets from a computer shop, scan the design and print it onto the paper on your home printer and iron it onto your fabric. You will need a printer that can print an A3 design for the project in this book.

Transfer sheets for colour laser copiers and colour laser printers

Laser copiers and printers use toner and heat (i.e. the copies are hot when they come out of the machine). The colour copiers are the machines usually found in copy or T-shirt printing shops.

Transfer sheets for inkjet printers

Inkjet printers use INK and NO heat (i.e. the copies are cold when they come out of the machine). These are the printers mostly used at home. You will need to purchase specially prepared fabric blocks for inkjet printers. These blocks ensure that the ink will not wash out once laundered.

Some transfers are hot peel paper, i.e. you need to peel the backing off whilst still hot. Some are cold peel paper – the opposite of the above.

Roses in silk and organza ribbon

A FEW POINTERS WHEN USING TRANSFER PAPER

Reverse the image

Your design will need to be reversed (a mirror image) before being copied onto the transfer paper.

When approaching a copy shop to do the transfer for you, they should automatically reverse the image before they print. If the copier does not have a "mirror image" function, you could make a transparency first and then reverse the transparency before making a copy on the transfer sheet.

When using your home computer, scanner and printer, you should be able to reverse the image on most scan, draw and paint applications.

Use the original design in this book

It is most important that you use the original watercolour from this book. A copy of the original (second generation copy) will mean that you lose detail and this will result in a very flat design with too much yellow or blue.

Prepare the fabric for printing

If you are not using prepared for printing (PFP) or prepared for dyeing (PFD) fabric, treat the fabric first to remove any dirt and finishes. See the section on fabric later in this chapter on page 15.

Ensure that your fabric is large enough to be stretched onto a frame. You will need at least 10cm (4") of border around your design to stretch it properly. A good size is 60 x 60cm (24 x 24") square.

Before using the heat transfer: press out any wrinkles with a hot iron. This will also remove any moisture in the fabric. The fabric must be smooth and dry to receive the transfer.

Preparing your heat transfer sheet

1. If you are taking a transfer home from the copy shop, place it between tissue paper or inside a plastic bag to protect it.
2. Cut the white, unprinted edge away, leaving rounded corners.

DOING A TRANSFER

The iron

Use an older model iron with no steam vents, if possible.

If using one with vents, remember to switch the steam off and to keep moving the iron slowly to get an even distribution of heat.

Set the temperature onto the highest heat that the fabric can handle. Allow enough time for the iron to heat up – about five minutes or so.

HEAT TRANSFER – PRINT, IRON, PEEL!

The surface

The surface should be smooth and firm to do a good transfer. Prepare your own surface as ironing boards are too soft. Use any smooth board that is slightly larger than the transfer sheet. Set it on a work table and pad with an old pillowcase or sheet. Make sure that the transfer fits on the board to prevent an ugly mark from forming if it overlaps the board.

The padding should be smooth with no folds or creases and it should be the same thickness throughout. Use the hot iron to press the padding on the board, until it is piping hot. The heated surface allows for a better transfer.

The transfer

Read about fabric on page 15. Centre the prepared fabric, right side up, on the heated surface. Place the transfer sheet right side down in the centre of the fabric.

Place the hot iron on the centre of the transfer, moving it slowly and applying as much pressure as you can for 20 to 30 seconds per section. Apply the heat as evenly as possible before moving on. Start in the centre and work in a circular movement towards the outside to prevent air bubbles from forming.

ABOUT TRANSFER PAPER

Transfer sheets – also called T-shirt transfers – are available from office supply stores, quilting, art and craft outlets, computer and printing shops. Some of these outlets will do the printing for you.

It is important to use the correct paper for the correct printer or copier. Laser and inkjet printers use different transfer paper because they operate differently. Carefully read the manufacturer's label on the paper.

If you use paper intended for an inkjet printer inside a laser copier or printer, it will melt the paper and damage the machine. Always check with your supplier which paper should be used in your machine.

Keep your arms straight and press down as hard as you can. Now iron the transfer once again, so the whole transfer is heated up – it must be hot in all areas before you peel it off. While the transfer is still hot, lift a corner to see if all or most of the colour is on the fabric. If not, iron again, and use more pressure and heat.

If the image looks good, start peeling the transfer while it is still hot. Hold the fabric down on the board and peel with an even tension from side to side or top to bottom. Don't peel across the bias of the fabric, as this will distort the fabric. If the paper does not peel easily because it has cooled down, reheat a section and peel as you heat.

THE SOLVENT METHOD

Transferring the coloured design onto fabric with the solvent method results in a less clear print, but it is cost-effective. **Caution:** Work in a well-ventilated area, away from foodstuff and children. Use white cotton or silk fabric. Ask the copy shop to enlarge and make a good photocopy of the design onto glossy paper so that the toner sits on top of the paper. The image should be reversed. Prepare the fabric and surface as for heat transfers; tape the corners of the photocopy on the fabric.

Use gloves and soak a ball of cotton wool in thinners. Apply liberally to the paper. Rub with the back of a spoon to get a good transfer. Lift one corner to check, and if happy with the amount of toner transferred, remove paper and leave fabric to dry. Iron to heat set. Rinse to get rid of the solvent.

TRACING THE LINE DRAWING

If you don't have access to colour-copying facilities or the printed panel, enlarge the line drawing on page 159 by 156% and trace it onto your fabric. Any fabric will do as long as you can see through it to do the tracing.

Lay the fabric on top of the photocopy and pin or tape in place. Use a sharp 2B pencil to carefully trace the design. Working on a light box or glass table with a light underneath it makes tracing easier.

Keep sharpening the pencil to ensure fine lines as the pencil does not wash out. The lines will be covered with the stitches and ribbon. Draw light lines and use a ruler for the straight lines. Excepting for the borders, draw 2mm ($\frac{1}{16}$") inside the leaves and flowers on the design. This prevents any pencil lines from showing once embroidered. You could also mark the position of small petals and roses with little dots.

About copy shops
Copy shops are available in most major centres and they can do the transfer for you.

Or you are welcome to look at www.dicraft.co.za for your nearest stockist to supply you with the printed panel.

Hint: Take care not to let the print shift, as this will give you a blurred image.

Roses in silk and organza ribbon

About fabric and backing fabric

A soft, smooth, medium-weight fabric with a relatively high thread count is a good choice for this kind of embroidery. The fabric should be strong enough to support the stitches in the design.

For colour transfers, fibre content is important. Pure cotton works best: it can withstand the high temperatures required for heat transfers. Avoid polycotton blends, which tend to make the transfer more plastic and therefore more difficult to insert the needle through.

Smooth surface, high thread count and colour of the fabric are important for a proper transfer. Rough, loosely woven fabric, although easier to work through, leads to loss of detail on the transfer and the loose weaves tend to pull out of shape too easily. You will soon get used to working with a large chenille needle, which makes a big enough hole for the ribbon to pass through easily. The best colour to use is white or off-white.

Darker shades tend to spoil the transfer as all the white detail in the image takes on the background colour. Make sure that the fabric is clean and free of wrinkles. It should be free of any sizing or starches, so it is a good idea to prewash in hot water with soap powder.

For tracing the line drawing, all that you would require is that the fabric complements the design, that it is strong enough to hold the stitches and that you are able to see the pattern through the fabric when tracing it.

About backing fabric

Before you start to embroider, an additional layer of fabric should be added to the back of your embroidery panel to stabilize and support it. Fine, soft, white muslin, lawn and polyester silk are all good choices. Ensure that the backing fabric is the same size as the embroidery block and that it is neither too thick nor too tight a weave. The layers are stretched onto a frame and you will stitch through both layers from the beginning.

Embroidery frames and hoops

A suitable frame or hoop greatly enhances your enjoyment of the finished piece.

About rectangular frames

Working on a rectangular wooden frame for this design is a good idea – the roses on the corners and sides would be covered by the customary round hoop. The size of the design is 29.03 x 38.2cm (11.43 x 15.039") and it should have a generous border of fabric around so that it fits easily onto a frame. The size of the fabric block, which the image is printed onto, is 60 x 60cm (23 x 23").

The rectangular frame should be larger than the printed image – this will allow enough space so the edge of the wooden frame won't be in the way whilst you stitch.

There are many kinds of frames: needlework frames, stretcher bars or bar frames, ratchet frames, scroll frames and lap frames. These are available from needlecraft stores and websites.

Popular products are the Evertite Stretcher Bar frames – also known as Evertite Stitchery Frames or Evertites – which have an adjustable tension, come in a number of sizes, and are obtainable from needlecraft outlets in the USA. I am sure that the frames are available in other countries too, and if you search for Evertite Stretcher Frames on Google, you may find a store or website that will post one on to you. Have a look at the article written by Mary Corbett on her website: www.needlenthread.com Search for: Evertite Stretcher Bar frames.

Wooden frames

You could ask your local framer to make a frame for you, like I do. Ask the framer to make a lightweight wooden frame measuring, from the outside of the frame, 37 x 49cm (14½ x 19"). The wood should be soft enough for you to push drawing pins (brass thumbtacks) into.

STRETCHING YOUR FABRIC ONTO THE FRAME

Before stretching the panel onto a frame, you will need to add a second layer of fabric on the back of your embroidery – see *about backing fabric* on page 15. You will stitch through both layers of fabric. The backing fabric acts as a stabiliser and it is easier to end off at the back. Place backing fabric on a flat surface; lay your embroidery panel on top, right side up. Tack the two layers along the edge, working through both layers to join them.

Hint: Another way to find a suitable frame is to purchase a ready-blocked artist's canvas which is about 49cm x 37cm (19 x 14½") in size. These are available from art and craft stores. Simply remove the canvas and if necessary, sandpaper the frame until it is smooth, before stretching your embroidery panel onto it.

Using brass thumbtacks or drawing pins

Use brass thumbtacks or drawing pins to secure the panel onto your frame. Place the frame on the right side of your embroidery panel and position frame until the panel is centred with equal parts of white showing along the sides. Use a pencil and draw the outline of the frame onto the white border of the fabric. The lines will help in the next step.

Place both layers of fabric on frame, positioning it so that pencil marks line up with the frame. Insert first tack in the centre of one edge; work to the corner and then to the other corner until first side is tacked down. Repeat on the opposite side of the frame, checking that the pencil line is straight. As you stretch, the lines will move further down the side of the frame. Pull gently on both layers of fabric as you tack to stretch the layers. Don't distort the fabric; a gentle, even tension is required.

Tack the third and fourth sides as you did above until layers are straightened firmly in the frame, but not so much that the fabric is warped.

Cover the tacks with masking tape so that your threads won't catch on them as you work.

> Hint: You could ask your framer or someone who is familiar with a staple gun or machine – also known as a trigger tacker – to stretch and staple the cloth to the frame. **DO NOT** try this yourself unless you are familiar with the stapler and you are aware of all the safety rules.

The frame can be attached to a stand, which is available from some needlecraft or quilting stores. Alternatively, lean part of the frame against the edge of your worktable or sofa, to prop it up whilst you embroider.

> Hint: The upside of using a rectangular frame is that you will be able to use it to display your work in.

Round hoops

A round 15cm (6") embroidery hoop is used for the small shapes which are made separately and then applied to your design, for example the butterflies and stumpwork leaves. It is also useful when making a single rose or panel in this book.

Getting started

17

About the ribbons

Pure silk ribbons were used to create the roses in this design. Choose silk taffeta ribbons for their crisp, smooth, lustrous fibre. This way your roses will look almost lifelike with petals that are as soft as they are in nature. Try to use the hand-painted ribbons so there is a variation in colour, with light and dark areas which will add shadows and highlights on the rose. I used my own range of ribbons in this book, and for your convenience, the codes are listed with each chapter in case you need them. These ribbons are available from needlecraft stores worldwide and you will find the list on my website www.dicraft.co.za by searching for stockists worldwide.

Hint: The ribbon looks quite coarse in the photographs, which are of such high quality that the camera has picked up the fibres of the silk. The ribbon is actually as smooth as silk.

Organza ribbon was used for the leaves of some roses and the butterfly wings. This ribbon is available from outlets worldwide. Do feel free to use ribbons of your own choice; as long as the ribbon is a fine, crisp, smooth taffeta silk and the organza not too rough a weave, the roses will turn out well.

Working with ribbon

Silk ribbon embroidery is surprisingly easy to master. Use silk ribbon just like any other thread or yarn, but take into consideration that it is softer and more fragile. Read more about *needles* on page 21 – it is essential to use a needle with a large eye, to make a big enough hole in the fabric, so that the ribbon does not snag or fold.

Use short lengths of ribbon: 30cm (12") lengths for 2 and 4mm ribbon, 20cm (8") lengths for 7 and 13mm ribbon. Too long a piece and the ribbon will fray as it is pulled through the fabric too often.

Threading ribbon

Thread needle and pierce the end that has just been threaded; pull the long tail to tighten the knot. Refer to *threading ribbon* on page 40.

To start the stitch
When starting with ribbon you have several choices:

a) Leave a small tail at the back and when you make your first or your second stitch, pierce the tail to secure it onto the fabric.

b) Or for the wider ribbons: secure tail with embroidery thread and stitches. This is a most effective method.

c) Or knot the 2 and 4mm ribbons as you would a thread. The texture of the design is busy enough to hide the bulkiness of the knot.

d) Or make a looped knot: Fold tail of the ribbon onto itself and pierce the fold with needle. Pull needle and ribbon through the fold to form a loop-like knot.

To end off
Leave 1cm (⅜") tail at the back; secure with small stitches. Trim tails for ease of stitching.

Hints on silk ribbon

Remember to use 20 to 30cm (8 to 12") lengths. Use 20cm (8") especially when working with 7 and 13mm silk ribbons.

Use your left thumb (or right thumb if you're left-handed) and hold the ribbon flat as you pull it to the back. Only let go once the stitch is almost done. This prevents the stitch from twisting or scrunching up. Otherwise work over a tapestry needle to support the ribbon until you have gently pulled it through the fabric.

Work with a gentle tension: ribbon should be handled lightly. Keep stitches loose and unfolded; allow the ribbon to spread to its full width on the fabric before starting the next stitch. If your tension is too tight and the needle too small, the ribbon will fold or scrunch up and the beautiful texture will be lost.

Form some stitches with flat ribbon and others with twisted ribbon for an interesting effect.

About ribbon stitch

Use a gentle tension and flatten the ribbon before making the ribbon stitch by running the side of the needle under the ribbon to iron out the creases. Insert a cotton earbud (or similar object) under the ribbon to push the ribbon outwards before forming the stitch. This helps to form a soft, rounded stitch.

To make a regular ribbon stitch: insert the needle in the middle of the ribbon's width. Work over a tapestry needle or your finger to form loose/puffed petals or leaves.

To make a ribbon stitch which curls to the right, insert the needle on the right-hand edge.

To make a ribbon stitch which curls to the left, insert the needle on the left-hand edge.

To make a twisted ribbon stitch: for an interesting leaf or petal, twist the ribbon before piercing it.

To make a cylindrical shape: twist the ribbon several times before piercing it.

To make a ribbon stitch with a curled-up tip: insert a spare tapestry needle into the loop that is formed as you take the ribbon to the back. Pull gently to lock the ribbon around the needle.

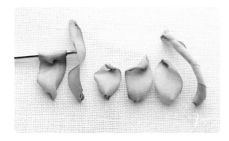

See how one stitch becomes a different shape, depending on where you insert the needle, and whether you twist it or not.

To form a looped ribbon stitch: don't pull the ribbon all the way to the back. This way, a loop will form which adds more texture.

SECURING, SHAPING STITCHES

Use one strand of matching thread and tiny stab stitches (short straight stitches) to secure the tip and the base of the stitch. This way, the ribbon will not pull out of shape when you make the adjoining stitch.

To shape a stitch, use tiny stab stitches along the edge of the ribbon, gently pulling it into position as you stitch.

Use straight stitches on top of a leaf to form the veins, gently pushing the edge of the ribbon into shape at the same time.

Use a cotton earbud or a tapestry needle to gently lift the stitch, if necessary.

WORKING WITH TWO NEEDLES

You will use one needle with ribbon to make the petal or leaf and another needle with thread to secure it. Always have one needle on the top of your work. If both needles are at the back of your work, they will become entangled.

MAKING HOLES IN FABRIC

To make a stitch with wider 7mm and 13mm ribbons, it is a good idea to make a hole in your fabric before you make the stitch. This way, the ribbon will not be damaged and it's easier to pull the ribbon through the fabric. Use a size 16 chenille needle; pull it all the way through the fabric. Then insert needle and ribbon through the hole. The ribbon opens up once the stitch is formed and covers the hole. When you use a stab stitch to secure the ribbon, pull the ribbon gently as you form the stitch to neaten the base of the petal or leaf.

Threads, fibres and needles

The beauty of creative embroidery is that you can use virtually any threads and woolly fibres, adding to the joy in stitching and to the visual appeal.

There is a vast choice of threads and fibres globally. In this book, I have used the DMC six-strand floss and the Rajmahal Art. silks which both have a lovely sheen and are freely available worldwide. The list is to be found in every chapter of this book. To add lustre, I used Kreinik blending filament and Madeira silver and gold metallic threads. Do, however, use whatever threads you feel like. The lists provided are merely a guideline for embroiderers who prefer to use the same codes as I did in this book.

The woolly fibres (see image on the right) used for the little birds and for some rose centres are available from needlecraft and felting outlets. You are also welcome to order these from my website: www.dicraft.co.za by searching for fibre.

NEEDLES

It is essential that you use the correct size needle for threads and ribbons. I have listed the needles and their sizes in each chapter of this book.

It is vital that the needle makes a large enough hole in the fabric for the ribbon to pass through without being snagged or damaged.

This way, the ribbon spreads to form a soft, open stitch instead of being scrunched up when pulled through a hole which is too small. The eye of the needle should be long enough for the ribbon to fit into. The needles to use for this kind of embroidery are:

Crewel/embroidery: a sharp, fine needle with a long, large eye. Use size 9 for the DMC, Kreinik and metallic threads and a size 10 for the Rajmahal Art.Silk.

Chenille: A thick needle with a sharp point and a long eye.

For:
- 13mm ribbon – use a size 16
- 7mm ribbon – use a size 18
- 4mm ribbon – use a size 20
- 2mm ribbon – use a size 22

Tapestry: same as chenille needle, but with a blunt tip. Use these needles to shape stitches. Useful as a support when forming loose, raised stitches – insert the needle under the stitch as it is formed.

Interesting effects

Make your design special. Personalise it with little touches like stumpwork and interesting finds.

Wire effects

To add dimension and structure to a leaf, wire can be added to form freestanding leaves which are raised off from the surface of the design. #0.38 beading wire is good, as are paper leaves available from craft shops. The paper leaf is attached to the back of a leaf which has been stitched and cut out. The wire then serves as the stalk of the leaf. You will learn more about this in the step-by-step instructions.

Jewellery and beads

A silver spider earring, purchased from a craft market or jewellery stores, adds character to your piece. Remove the butterfly stop from the earring and use a pair of pliers to bend the shaft backwards. Insert it into the fabric and secure with tiny stitches. Round, oval and half-round beads add dimension and you will learn how to use these in the chapters that follow.

Finds

This is the collective word for anything that you find and use to enhance your design. Experiment and use creative ideas to add your own personal touch. Use raffia to make a nest, wool fibre to create a feathery texture, pieces of textured wool or French ribbon to make stems and branches. Later on, in the chapters that follow, I will show you how.

Stems from imitation flowers

Cut a piece of stem from an imitation flower and wrap it with ribbon. It adds a lovely texture to your design, with lifelike results. You will learn about this in chapter 2 and other chapters in this book.

Metallic threads

A translucent blending filament, such as the Kreinik 032, is perfect for adding highlights on leaves, roses and little birds. Gold and silver threads add a luxurious texture to the borders. A list of what I used is included with every chapter.

Other tools and requirements

- **Scissors:** Small, sharp embroidery scissors are a must.
- **Wire-cutters or nail clippers:** to trim wire.
- **Needle grabber:** thin piece of rubber to help pull needle through.
- **Clean hands:** Wet wipes or a damp face cloth close by. You will also need to wipe your needle after dipping it into the glue stick and a damp face cloth comes in handy.
- **Floss box:** A plastic box to store threads, with plastic cards to wind the thread onto. Soft cardboard rolls or soft plastic Spooly (see picture below) to keep your silk or French ribbons neat and tidy

- **Large plastic bag** or pillowcase to store your embroidery.
- **Leather or steel thimble:** If you prefer using one.
- **Daylight, magnifiers and lighting:** With a comfortable chair and worktable. It is best to have all your threads and ribbons in front of you whilst you stitch. Sit with your chair further back than normal, allowing the frame to rest on the table's edge. This free space allows easy access to the back of your work and prevents a stiff neck and shoulders from holding the hoop. An embroidery stand is also a good idea and it is available from most quilting stores.
- **Pens and pencils:** You will need a blue water-soluble pen, black waterproof pigment ink pen and a 2B pencil.

- **Glue:** A glue stick (similar to what the kids use for school projects) is ideal for curling petals and other applications in this book. The glue should be non-toxic, solvent and acid-free and only use the glue stick – not liquid glue. Pritt ™ is made by Henkel in Germany and it is available worldwide. Glitter glue is useful for the butterfly wings.
- **Water-soluble fabric and anti-fray agent:** Both are available from machine embroidery shops and needlecraft stores. Use a **clear** liquid anti-fray agent. Test that it dries clear. Water-soluble fabric looks like a fine plastic film and it dissolves in water.

HANDY RULER (cm/inch)

Millimeters	Inches
3mm	1/8"
6mm	1/4"
13mm	1/2"
16mm	5/8"
19mm	3/4"
22mm	7/8"
25mm	1"
38mm	1 1/2"
44mm	1 3/4"
51mm	2"
64mm	2 1/2"

Getting started

23

WHERE DO I START?
The following sequence works well:

Step 1
Transfer design as explained on page 10 or purchase a printed panel from www.dicraft.co.za or from your nearest stockist.

Step 2
Choose ribbons and threads as listed in each chapter.

Step 3
Collect the necessary materials and equipment.

Step 4
Choose interesting effects that you wish to add to your design.

Step 5
Stretch your design in an embroidery frame.

> *Hint: Read handy hint below about keeping your work clean.*

Step 6
Cover the design with a sheet of cellophane. Cut out a window for the section that you will be working on and replace the sheet of cellophane whenever necessary. It is a good idea to start in the top left-hand corner (or top right-hand corner if you are left-handed)

Step 7
The best part: Find your favourite chair and settle in to embroider.

Handy hints and other good tips

Keeping your work clean
To keep your work clean, use the window method: Cut a block of inexpensive white fabric which is the same size as your embroidery cloth. Place it on top of your embroidery cloth and secure it on your frame. Carefully cut out a window – be careful not to cut your embroidery cloth – using the edge of the design as a guide.

Ending off tails at the back
For a neat finish and to make the embroidery process easier, always secure all the tails at the back and trim the excess ribbon and thread.

Other good tips
Trace shapes onto tracing paper before tracing them onto ribbon. Don't work directly from book as it may mark your book.

Keep your scraps of thread in a small box on your work table and your needles in a pincushion so that they don't get lost.

Remember to replace the cap on your glue stick, so it does not dry out.

Techniques

Making rose petals

Rose petals made with silk taffeta ribbon are almost lifelike in quality. There are loose petals which are flat and others which are curled. Some are folded and gathered, some are rolled and gathered, others are simply rolled. All of these techniques you will learn in this book.

MAKING LOOSE, FLAT PETALS
The templates are provided with each chapter and these are traced onto the 32mm silk taffeta ribbon.

Place ribbon on the tracing (read *other good tips* on page 24). Use a blue water-soluble pen; trace shapes onto ribbon. Make a dotted line if ribbon moves about too much.

Cut out the shapes, one by one, with sharp embroidery scissors keeping track whether it is an A, B or C petal. The shape will change slightly: this is not a problem at all.

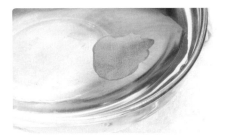

Place petals, one by one, into a bowl of water, still keeping track whether it is an A, B or C petal. This will dissolve the blue outline on the petal. A minute or two is sufficient.

Place shapes on a towel, in groups, alongside each other. Cut small squares of paper and mark the groups according to their symbol: A, B, C... allow time to dry.

Apply clear anti-fray agent (read more about this on page 23). Wet ribbon completely to prevent water marks. Allow time to dry.

The petals are now ready to be curled or to be placed directly onto your design. Handle with care to prevent fraying of the edges.

MAKING CURLED PETALS

Curled rose petals add to the authentic appearance of the roses. Some petals are curled before they are added, others are curled afterwards. I will show you how in the chapters that follow.

Note: Do read about the glue stick which you will use to curl petals on pages 23 and 24.

Prepare loose, flat petals as shown on the previous page. Wait for them to dry. Keep them in groups for easy reference as you will need to know whether they are A or B petals when placing the petals onto your design in the step-by-step instructions.

Use size 18 tapestry needle: dip it into the glue stick. Use sticky part of needle to roll up the edge. Press the edge of ribbon against needle and start rolling until the petal is curled. Remove the needle; wipe it (and your hands) with a damp cloth and repeat for the opposite edge.

To form a petal with a blunt tip, make another roll on the sharp end of the petal. Gently remove the needle, wipe your hands and the needle.

Hint: Keep wiping your hands and your needle as it is difficult to work with sticky hands.

Make petals of different shapes: some curled twice, some curled again to create an interesting rose.

Some petals are curled once across the tip – see the Remember Me Rose in chapter 9. For Rose Gaujard in chapter 2, the petals are curled after they have been stitched onto the design.

Some curled petals are added onto a woolly centre, others onto a folded rose – with lifelike results.

MAKING FOLDED AND GATHERED PETALS

For some roses, a length of ribbon is folded in half or in thirds, and then gathered with a lovely effect. I will show you how, for example, in chapter 5.

Fold 32mm ribbon in half; iron it flat with your fingertips. Make running stitches along the edges. Lightly gather the ribbon as shown in the chapters that follow.

Or fold the ribbon in thirds so that the top fold is about 1cm (⅜") wide. Make running stitches along the folded edge and gather. See more about this in chapter 5.

The folded and gathered petals are used for the Brandy Rose on page 70 but you could also use them for the Blanche Lafitte Rose in chapter 8 on page 88.

MAKING ROLLED AND GATHERED PETALS

A short length of ribbon is rolled and gathered to create plump petals – it is a wonderful technique which I will show you how to use in the chapters that follow.

Refer to the instructions in the chapter for the rose that you are making. Cut a length of 32mm ribbon. Thread up with matching thread and make a knot at the long end. Apply glue on one corner. Read about this glue on page 23.

Use an 18 tapestry needle: roll up the sticky part of the ribbon. Use your fingers to press the edge of the ribbon against the needle and start rolling. Work quickly before the glue dries. Secure the roll with a small stab stitch.

Gently move the tapestry needle out of the roll, wipe your hands and needle with a damp cloth. Use the same thread and make small running stitches along the edge. The stitches should be about 3mm (⅛") in size.

Leave the thread in the needle and glue the opposite corner. Roll the corner with the tapestry needle as you did before.

Catch the edge of the rolled ribbon with the needle and thread. Remove the tapestry needle while glue is still damp; leave thread in the needle. Wipe hands and tapestry needle.

Pull the thread to lightly gather the ribbon and place the petal between the others. Secure in place with the same thread and tiny stab stitches. I will show you how in the chapters that follow.

OTHER METHODS TO USE FOR MAKING PETALS

There are many other ways of making rose petals and I will show you how in the chapters that follow. You will learn how to make roses by rolling up ribbon and by making looped or round petals.

Rolling lengths of ribbon

Insert a length of ribbon as shown in the step-by-step instructions for the specific rose, leaving a length of ribbon on top of your work. Dip tapestry needle into the glue stick and roll up the ribbon, using your fingers to press the edge of the ribbon against the needle. Roll until the petal is short enough for the rose. Secure as shown in the chapters that follow.

Making looped petals

Working over the tapestry needle (or your fingertip) creates softly raised petals. Make the stitches loose and looped. A second loop will form if you don't pull the ribbon all the way to the back – this adds more petals on the rose.

Hint: Before using the wider 7 and 13mm ribbons, read about making holes in fabric on page 20.

Making plump, round petals

To make round roses, cut out circular shapes from 32mm ribbon, gather them and apply to your design. Add stamens on top to flatten the shape. I will show you how in chapter 13.

For plump petals: make a French knot and cover it with ribbon stitch. You will learn how in chapter 6.

Roses in silk and organza ribbon

MAKING HALF-ROLLED PETALS

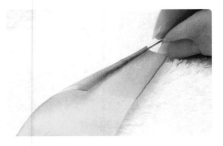

Cut a length of 32mm ribbon; use a matching thread with knot at the long end. Glue the one end of the ribbon (as you did for the rolled and gathered petals on page 27) and use an 18 tapestry needle to roll the end.

Insert the needle into the rolled end of the petal – the pointed end – and secure the edge of the roll with a stab stitch.

Remove the tapestry needle and wipe your hands and the needle.

> Note: There is no need to make running stitches along the straight edge of the half-rolled petals.

Leave the thread on the needle and make folds on the end of the ribbon that is not curled. Three folds, one on top of another, are sufficient.

Holding the folds, wrap the petal around the centre of a rose as shown in chapter 9.

Secure the petal with small stab stitches as shown in the step-by-step instructions ...

... or, as shown in chapter 11 and 8, gently lift the rose petals and secure the pointed end between the petals with a few stab stitches. Curl petal around the rose; secure the other end between the petals. To make more folds on this petal, once it is secured, use the tapestry needle and gently run it across the petal to form the creases.

The rose centres

You will learn several methods of how to make the centre of a rose – some roses are made with round little balls, others with beads or yellow French knots and pistil stitch.

Note: See page 41 for the illustration of the folded ribbon rose.

FOLDED RIBBON ROSE CENTRE

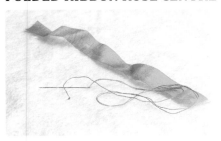

Cut a length of ribbon and use a matching thread with a knot at the long end. When using 13mm ribbon for a small centre, don't fold it at all.

For a larger centre, use 32mm ribbon. Make a small fold as advised in the chapter, or fold it in half. Follow the instructions for the specific rose in the step-by-step instructions.

I will show you how to make a folded ribbon rose with a 32mm ribbon which has a small fold. Fold the end to make a corner.

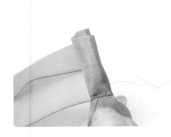

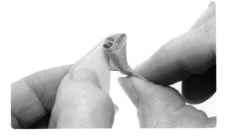

1. Roll the end five times and use tiny stab stitches to secure the bottom edge of the roll. Keep the tail on the left at all times.

2. Leave thread hanging; fold the ribbon towards you at an angle of 45 degrees. The tail should be hanging downwards.

3. Hold the tail, lifting it so that it is level with the centre; wrap it around the centre until the folded part is used up. The tail is back on the left.

Techniques

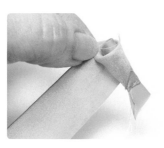

4. Pinch the top of the rose and hold it as you secure the folds with tiny stab stitches, working halfway up the rose. Use a gentle tension so as not to flatten the centre. Make four or five stitches to secure.

5. Repeat step 2 and then 3.

Remember to lift the tail so the folded part is level with the centre of the rose, and make sure that the tail is either hanging down or that it is (always) on your left.

6. When you reach the end of the ribbon, make a fold ...

7. ... and secure it near the base of the rose. If there is still enough thread on the needle, use it to secure the petals in the next step. See chapters 2, 9, 11 and 14.

Remember, this is only the centre of the rose, petals will be added around it to make a full rose. Trim the tail of the rose.

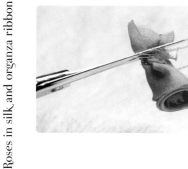

HOW TO ENLARGE THE FOLDED RIBBON ROSE

If you would like to enlarge the centre slightly, add a second layer of ribbon around the rose. Use a 15cm length of the 32mm ribbon, fold it in half and wrap it around the centre, repeating the process.

Fold the end; secure in place with small stab stitches.

Wrap around centre; make a fold.

Wrap again with a gentle tension and end off as you did before.

TWIRLED RIBBON ROSE

The twirled ribbon rose is a wonderful stitch to use for making rose centres and buds. See page 41 in the stitch gallery for the illustration of this stitch.

1. Come up in the centre of the rose; gently twist the needle to form a neat tubular shape.

2. Insert needle back into the fabric ...

3. ... twirl the ribbon with your fingers; hold the twirls whilst pulling ribbon to the back.

4. Hold the twirls gently to stabilise them ...

5. ... pull very softly until a rose is formed. Pull gently until you are happy with the size of the rose.

6. Use tiny stab stitches, French knots or beads in the centre to secure the rose. See more about this in the chapters that follow.

ABOUT THE CALYX, LEAVES AND STEMS

Calyx

The round tube of a calyx is made with a covered bead or French knot. I will show you how in the chapters that follow. The green sepals are made with ribbon stitch; some are flat, others are twisted. Larger sepals are made separately, rolled and secured onto the design. See chapters 2 and 9.

Stems

In chapters 2, 9, 11 and 14 you will learn how to cover stems of imitation flowers with lifelike results ...

... and in chapters 3 and 13 you will learn how to make branches and stems with French ribbon and wool.

Leaves

Some leaves are stumpwork leaves, which are made separately with silk and organza ribbon and then secured onto the design. In chapter 7 you will learn how to combine these textures with a lustrous effect.

Other stumpwork leaves are made in thread and then cut out and applied to the design. You will learn this technique in chapter 2.

The leaves of several roses and the rose hips are made in ribbon stitch and embellished with thread. I will show you how in the chapters that follow.

Roses in silk and organza ribbon

ABOUT ROSEBUDS, ROSE HIPS AND SPENT ROSES

Rosebuds
In the chapters that follow, you will learn how to roll ribbon to make a gorgeous elongated bud …

… and how to use layers of ribbon to make a large bud; how to use twirled stitches to create round, plump buds and how to make small rosebuds with simple stitches.

Rose hips and spent roses
You will learn how to create realistic rose hips by covering oval beads … and how to make the stamens and calyxes of the spent roses.

ABOUT THE BUTTERFLIES AND BIRDS
In the chapters that follow you will learn how to use iridescent fibres for butterfly wings and woolly fibres to create a feathery texture for the little birds.

Butterflies
You will learn how to make stumpwork wings for Purple Emperors with sheer organza ribbon …

… and Pearl Spotted Emperors

… and in chapter 4 I will show you how to make a Fig Tree Blue with organza and fabric.

Birds
Learn how to make a Blue Tit with woolly fibre, covered with stitches …

… and a Golden Breasted Bunting

… and a happy little Willow Warbler alongside his nest. Enjoy yourself!

Techniques

Stitch Gallery and Stitch Techniques

Stitches

Back stitch

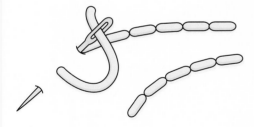

Blanket stitch

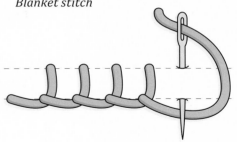

Chain stitch

Couching

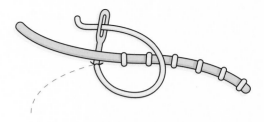

Detached buttonhole stitch

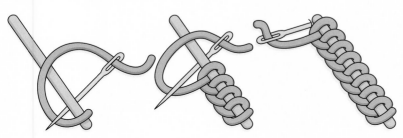

Long and short buttonhole stitch

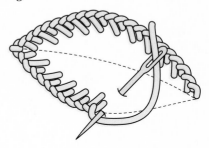

Detached chain (Lazy daisy)

Long and short stitch

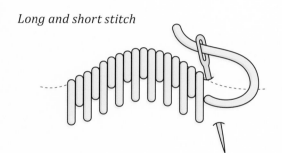 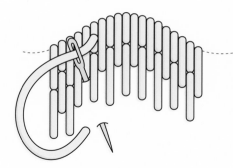

Loop stitch

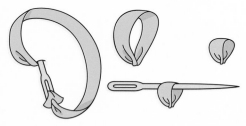

Fly stitch

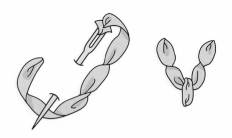

Overcast stitch

French knot

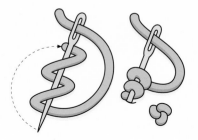

Running stitch

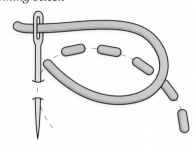

Pistil stitch

Split stitch

Stab stitch

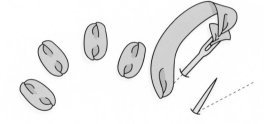

Ribbon stitch

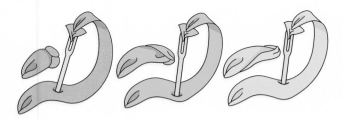

Straight stitch

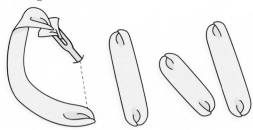

See more *about ribbon stitch* on page 19

Ribbon stitch – loose and puffed

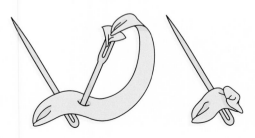

Twisted ribbon stitch

Ribbon stitch with curled up tip

  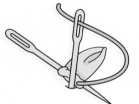

Stem stitch

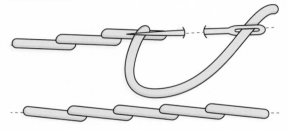

Stem stitch filling

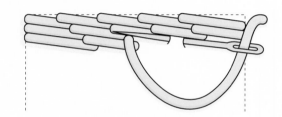

Whipped back stitch

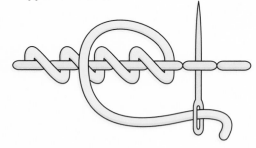

Whipped back stitch: double row

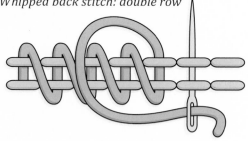

Twisted/twirled straight stitch

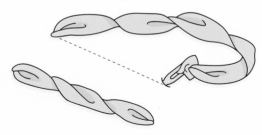

Whipped chain stitch

Whipped stem stitch

Threading ribbon

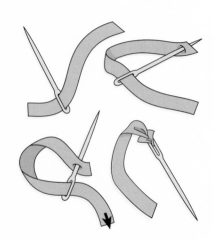

Stitch Techniques

Folded ribbon rose centre

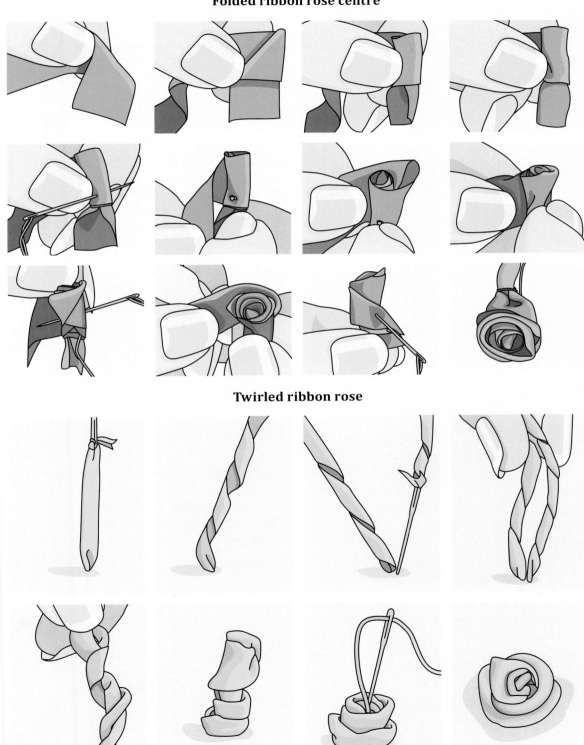

Twirled ribbon rose

The borders

To add structure, and to enhance the roses, embroider a border around your roses.

Creating borders and trellises

Depending on your project, embroider a border or trellis which will enhance and add structure. The borders should be stitched before you make the roses.

Use one or two strands of thread in soft shades of grey and brown. Cotton, rayon and silk thread are good choices. Silver and gold metallic threads, wound around the stitches, add a touch of glamour.

Select from the following stitches which are listed alphabetically in the stitch gallery on page 36:

Back stitch, blanket stitch, fly stitch, French knots, pistil stitch, split stitch, stem stitch, straight stitch and whipped chain stitch. Add a bead to form the dots.

In some instances – like the rose below – a border would not be required.

Chapter 2

Rose Gaujard, Golden Lace and Elina Rose

Actual size of the roses

Rose Gaujard

You will need

RIBBON

Di van Niekerk's silk ribbons

	7mm colour 24
	13mm colour 142
	13mm colour 108
	32mm colour 108
	4mm colour 17

THREAD

Use one strand of thread, unless suggested otherwise.

DMC six-strand embroidery floss

	3803
	523
	934
	642
	3687

Rajmahal Art.Silk

	745

Kreinik blending filament

	032

NEEDLES

Chenille size 16	
Chenille size 18	
Embroidery size 9	
Embroidery size 10	
Tapestry size 18	

OTHER

- 2 paper leaves on dark purple wire. See page 51
- Round necklace bead 5 to 6mm (³⁄₁₆")
- Anti-fray agent and fabric glue stick. See page 23
- Blue water-soluble pen. See page 23
- Black waterproof pigment ink pen. See page 23
- 15cm (6") embroidery hoop
- A block of white cotton fabric 20cm (8") square

STITCHES USED

Stitches are listed alphabetically in the stitch gallery on page 36.

> *Note: Read more about ribbon stitch on pages 19-20.*

Back stitch, folded ribbon rose, long and short buttonhole stitch, long and short stitch, ribbon stitch, running stitch, straight/stab stitch and whipped back stitch.

The stem

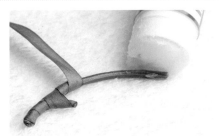

Bend the stem into shape; use the same thread to secure it onto the design with tiny stab stitches. Change to the pink 3687 thread; make thorns in straight/stab stitch. Insert the needle into the ribbon on the stem and go back into the fabric a short distance away.

This rose stem is made from a stem of an imitation flower – with authentic results. Cut a piece with wire-cutters to fit on the design. Glue one end of the stem and start wrapping it with the green 7mm silk ribbon. Before reaching the other end, add some glue and wrap the ribbon to cover the stem completely. Working backwards again, cover the stem a second time. Use the green 523 thread and tiny stab stitches to secure the ribbon onto the stem.

The rose

Make the rose petals

Use the 32mm pink ribbon and read: *making loose, flat petals* on page 25 and *other good tips* on page 24. Trace the petal shapes on the right. Trace six to eight small and six to eight large petals. For a plumper rose, trace extra petals: 12 small and 16 large petals in total.

Hint: Utilise the shading on the ribbon, including the marks which will form the veins of the petal. Trace some petals onto a pale section of ribbon and others onto a darker part, to create realistic petals.

Hint: Use very sharp embroidery scissors to cut the petals. They don't need to be exactly the same as the shapes below and they do change shape once cut and dried.

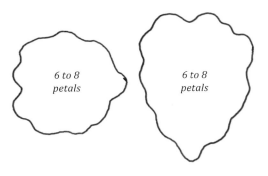

6 to 8 petals

6 to 8 petals

Templates to trace

Make the folded centre

Make the centre of the rose using the *folded ribbon rose* method on page 31. Depending on how large you would like the centre to be, cut a 15 to 20cm (6 to 8") length of pink 13mm ribbon. Use 3687 thread to secure the folded rolls. Trim the tails and place the centre aside to use later.

Add the petals

Use 3687 thread; secure a large petal with tiny stab stitches. Use three or four stitches per petal, stitching 5mm (³⁄₁₆") from the edge.

Add three more petals, using a stitch to scrunch the petals up slightly; make a stitch, and as you insert the needle into the ribbon, move the ribbon to form a fold.

Read *about ribbon stitch* on page 19. Make four small petals at the base of the stem. Use the pink 13mm ribbon, come up alongside the stem and leave a short tail at the back of your work. Secure the tail with the pink thread and trim tails at the back. Make loose, puffed ribbon stitches by stitching over a tapestry needle and working over the green stem.

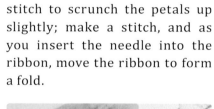

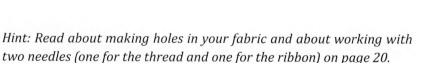

Hint: Read about making holes in your fabric and about working with two needles (one for the thread and one for the ribbon) on page 20.

Add the centre

Place the centre on top of the petals. To enlarge it slightly, read *how to enlarge the folded ribbon rose* on page 32. Add a second layer of ribbon around the rose. Use a 15cm (6") length of the pink 32mm ribbon, fold it in half and wrap it around the centre as shown on page 32.

Place the centre on the rose and stitch along the base with two stab stitches. It will be secured properly with more stitches a little later.

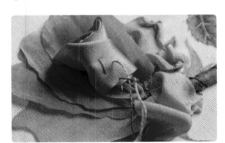

Add more petals

Lift the centre and some petals; add two or three small petals. Use the stitch to make folds in the ribbon if the petal is too long. Secure the centre along the base so that it does not move about too freely. Use a gentle tension so as not to flatten the centre of the rose.

Make the sepals

Change to green 7mm ribbon and make three small sepals in ribbon stitch, twisting the ribbon to form curved shapes. Work with a gentle tension from the stem outwards. Use green 523 thread and tiny stab stitches to secure sepals along the tip and base. Read *securing, shaping stitches* on page 20.

Add more petals

Use the remaining petals (small and large) and form the front part of the rose. Use pink thread and tiny stab stitches at the base of each petal. Only a few stitches are necessary – the petals will be folded over and secured properly a little later when you flip them over to lie on top of the centre of the rose.

Add more petals, using needle and thread to scrunch the petal up slightly; make a stitch and, as you insert the needle into the ribbon, move the ribbon to form a fold.

Keep adding petals, stitching them in place, folding them over onto the centre, securing them with tiny stitches, working through all the layers of ribbon.

This is a view from the top of the rose to show you how lifelike the petals appear to be.

The ribbon looks quite rough in these photographs as the pictures are of such high quality that the camera has picked up the fibres of the silk ribbon. The ribbon is actually silky smooth and has a lustre which is not visible here – exactly like the petals of a real rose.

When you add the next layer, push the first layer of petals forward and secure them onto the centre with tiny stab stitches along the base. Insert the needle into the centre and use a gentle tension so as not to flatten the folded centre.

Hint: Only stitch along the lower end (the base) of the petal. Add as many petals as you like.

Once you are happy with the amount of petals, shape them with your fingers, so that they curve around the centre. Use stitches to hold the contour, stitching through all layers to secure and shape.

Roses in silk and organza ribbon

48

Make the calyx

Add a round necklace bead to form the tube of the calyx. The bead fits just above the stem. Stitch through all layers to secure bead with three stitches. The bead should not move around too freely.

Use green 13mm ribbon and cut a piece long enough to be tucked around the bead. Use 523 thread and tiny stab stitches to stitch the ribbon around the bead. Use a gentle tension to tuck the ribbon in. Add a second layer of ribbon for a smooth finish.

Hint: You could also use same green ribbon to cover the bead with ribbon stitch, as you would with the rose hips on page 105.

Make the sepals

Use green 13mm ribbon and cut a piece which is 4 to 5cm (1½ to 2") long, depending on the size of your rose. Use 523 thread; make small running stitches along one raw edge. Leave thread on the needle; use glue stick to moisten the other raw end. Use a tapestry needle to curl up the end as shown. Remove needle before the glue dries.

Gather the thread; make tiny stab stitches to secure the gathered end near the bead. Stitch the sharp end onto the rose with small stab stitches, working through all the layers.

Hint: The stitches also help to enhance the roundness of this part of the rose. Repeat for the remaining two sepals and trim any frayed ends.

Curl and adjust the petals
Apply glue to the tapestry needle – see about working with this glue on page 26 – and curl the edge of the petals for a realistic effect. Use the tapestry needle; adjust the pink ribbon stitches. See the main picture of the rose at the beginning of this chapter.

The leaves

The leaves are made by using a stumpwork technique: they are made separately, cut out, and attached onto the design. You could, however, use green 13mm silk ribbon and ribbon stitch as shown in the rose on page 42. To prepare the stumpwork leaves: use the black pen to trace the shapes on page 51 (including the numbers) onto a block of white cotton fabric. You could also order the stumpwork panel, printed in full colour, from your nearest stockist or from my website www.dicraft.co.za by searching for stumpwork shapes.

Stretch the fabric in a 15cm (6") hoop and thread up with 3803 thread. Work along edge of the leaf in long and short buttonhole stitch.

Hint: When starting a stitch, come up 3mm (⅛") away from the edge or along the centre vein, then the knots won't be in the way when you cut out the leaf a little later.

Use long and short buttonhole stitch and work from the tip of the leaf to the base; end off. Start at the tip again; work the other side, noting the angle of the stitches, which should face towards the veins of the leaf. End off by running your thread under stitches at the back.

Use 523 thread and form the veins in back stitch. Use the same thread to whip the stitches for a raised effect.

Change to 934 thread and, working close to the centre vein, form a dark green patch in long and short stitch. Note how the stitches face towards the base of the leaf. Change to the 523 thread; make light green patches in long and short stitch, inserting the needle between the dark green stitches for a smooth finish.

Repeat with 642 thread; form the light patches on the outer edge. Use the shiny 032 thread to add highlights with straight stitches between the green ones. Change to 745 thread; fill in the dark pink edges in long and short stitch, working between the green stitches.

Chapter 2

Complete the leaves

Apply anti-fray agent along the edge of the leaves. Note the numbers and cut out the leaves, taking care not to cut the stitches. Lay each leaf on a piece of paper which is numbered according to the leaves.

Hint: Use the black waterproof pen to colour in the white bits showing along the edge of the leaf.

A quick way to add a wire stalk is to use paper leaves which are found at craft shops. The two leaves at the end of the stalks (leaves 1 and 6) have wired stalks. Cut the paper leaf to fit onto your leaf. Use the 642 thread and secure it onto the back of your leaf with tiny stab stitches, working through all the layers.

Make a hole in the fabric near the stem with a 16 chenille needle. Insert the wire into the fabric and after bending it at the back, secure the wire with tiny stab stitches. Trim the excess wire with wire-cutters.

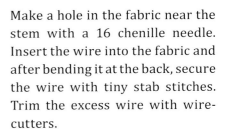

Use the thread and tiny stab stitches to secure the remaining leaves, allowing the tips to stand free for a lovely three-dimensional effect.

Make the small leaves at the base of the wired stalks with the green 4mm ribbon: use straight or ribbon stitch.

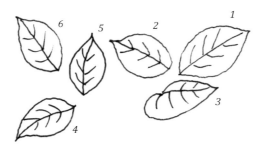

Templates to trace

OTHER IDEAS

Some roses are perfect for jewelry box lids and pieces to be framed behind glass: a beautiful card, a treasured piece of wearable art, a piece of a crazy quilting, an embroidered picture ...

If you would like to make a more durable rose, trace the petal and do not apply anti-fray. Singe the edges of the petal on a candle flame. Hold the petal with a forceps or tweezers and have a bowl of water nearby to insert the petal into if it catches alight.

Note: This can only be done with pure silk ribbon – any artificial fibres will melt. The darker the ribbons the better as the burned edges are not as visible.

Golden Lace

You will need

RIBBON

Di van Niekerk's silk ribbons

 4mm colour 33

7mm colour 99

THREAD

Use one strand of thread, unless suggested otherwise.

DMC six-strand embroidery floss

 523

Rajmahal Art.Silk

 841

45

NEEDLES

Chenille size 18

Chenille size 20

Embroidery size 9

Embroidery size 10

Tapestry size 18

STITCHES USED

Stitches are listed alphabetically in the stitch gallery on page 36.

> Note: Read more about ribbon stitch on pages 19-20.

French knot, loop stitch, ribbon stitch, stem stitch, straight/stab stitch, twirled ribbon rose and whipped stem stitch.

The stems and leaves

Use the 523 thread; make stems with stem stitch. Whip the stitches for a rounded effect. Change to the green 4mm ribbon and make the leaves in ribbon stitch, working from stems and roses outwards.

Use green thread and tiny stab stitches on tip and base of leaves to secure the stitch and end off at the back. Change to brown thread and use straight stitch to form the veins on the leaves.

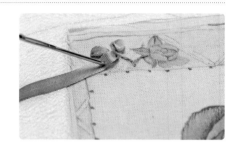

The roses

Thread up with the yellow ribbon; come up in the centre of the rose.

Hint: Read about making holes in fabric on page 20, as this will help with the twirled technique that follows. Use the yellow thread to secure the tail at the back of your work; come up and place needle and thread on top of your work.

Read about making a *twirled ribbon rose* on page 33. Twirl the ribbon and insert it nearby (or back into) the same hole. As you pull the ribbon to the back, hold the twirls to stabilize them. Pull very gently until a rose is formed.

Use yellow thread and tiny stab stitches to secure the centre of the rose. With a gentle tension, so as not to flatten the rose, make a few French knots with brown or yellow thread, wrapping the thread twice around needle.

Use yellow ribbon; make three ribbon stitches for the petals. Working from the centre outwards, form loose and puffed stitches. Use yellow thread and tiny stab stitches to secure petals at the tip to stabilise the stitch.

Repeat and make a twirled centre for the second rose. For the rose petals, make one ribbon stitch and three or four loop stitches. Working over a tapestry needle, hold the loop until you have secured it with yellow thread and tiny stab stitches. To form a closed rose, use stab stitches to secure the loop onto the centre of the rose.

Roses in silk and organza ribbon

Elina Rose

You will need

RIBBON

Di van Niekerk's silk ribbons

13mm colour 24

13mm colour 77 (x 2)

THREAD

Use one strand of thread, unless suggested otherwise.

DMC six-strand embroidery floss

3362

453

728

Rajmahal Art.Silk

226

96

91

NEEDLES

Chenille size 16

Chenille size 18

Embroidery size 9

Embroidery size 10

Tapestry size 13

STITCHES USED

Stitches are listed alphabetically in the stitch gallery on page 36.

> *Note: Read more about ribbon stitch on pages 19-20.*

French knot, loop stitch, ribbon stitch, straight/stab stitch and whipped stem stitch.

The stem and the leaves

Thread up with green thread and make the stem in whipped stem stitch. Insert needle under and over the stitches to form a rounded stem. Whip for a second time to form a thick stem.

Use green 13mm ribbon; make leaves in ribbon stitch. Use green thread and back stitch to form the central veins. Change to straight stitch for the other veins, using the stitch to shape the leaves at the same time. Change to the 226 thread and add a few dark grey veins in straight stitch.

The rose

Use cream 13mm ribbon; make seven petals in ribbon stitch. Work over a tapestry needle to form raised petals. Read about *making holes in fabric,* about *working with two needles* and about *securing, shaping stitches* on page 20. Use white thread and tiny stab stitches to secure the petals.

Make a second layer of petals, inserting the needle between the previous stitches. Be careful not to insert the needle into the stitches of the previous row as this will distort them. Gently move the petal out of the way and insert the needle into the fabric. Make five or six petals; secure with white thread and tiny stab stitches, fastening the tails at the back as well.

Make three loop stitches in the centre, working over a tapestry needle. If necessary, use a small pair of pliers or a needle gripper to gently pull the needle through the fabric. Secure each loop, as you did before.

Use 453 thread; make the stamens with French knots, wrapping thread three times around the needle. Use the 91 thread and make light yellow stamens in the same way. Change to the 3362 thread; make a green knot in the very centre. Finally, add dark yellow stamens with 728 thread, as you did above.

Wisteria *(Wisteria floribunda)* and Blue Tit *(Cyanistes caeruleus)*

Actual size of the Wisteria and bird

Wisteria

You will need

RIBBON

Di van Niekerk's silk ribbons

2mm colour 21

4mm colour 33

4mm colour 64

4mm colour 78

THREAD

Use one strand of thread, unless suggested otherwise.

DMC six-strand embroidery floss

809

840

Rajmahal Art.Silk

226

NEEDLES

Chenille size 20

Chenille size 22

Embroidery size 9

Embroidery size 10

Tapestry size 18

OTHER

• Brown French ribbon or yarn for the branch below the bird

STITCHES USED

Stitches are listed alphabetically in the stitch gallery on page 36.

> Note: Read more about ribbon stitch on pages 19-20.

Back stitch, chain stitch, French knot, ribbon stitch, stem stitch, straight/stab stitch and whipped back stitch.

The brown stems

Make the stems in whipped back stitch. Use brown 2mm ribbon and make back stitches which are about 3mm (⅛") long. Whip each stitch on your return journey, inserting needle under and over the stitch two or three times. Keep ribbon as flat as possible for a neat finish.

Insert the brown yarn into tapestry needle and wind it under and over the stitches of the stem, securing it with the grey thread and tiny stab stitches every cm (⅜") or so.

The leaves and flowers

Use green ribbon and make leaves in ribbon stitch. Use thread 226; secure each leaf with a straight stitch and make the grey stem between the leaves in stem stitch. Use brown thread to form the curved stem of the Wisteria in chain or stem stitch. Add French knots on top of and alongside the stem, wrapping thread three times around needle.

Change to 64 ribbon; make the flowers with French knots, wrapping ribbon once around the needle.

Cover knot with a ribbon stitch, inserting needle at an angle to tuck the ribbon around the knot. Use blue thread and tiny stab stitches to secure and to shape the stitches. Read about *securing, shaping stitches* on page 20. Further down the flower, change to the 78 ribbon and repeat. End off at the tip with a petite flower, by making a three-wrap French knot with the blue thread.

Blue Tit

You will need

THREAD

Use one strand of thread, unless suggested otherwise.

DMC six-strand embroidery floss

368

3807

Rajmahal Art.Silk

96

226

25

91

521

Kreinik blending filament

032

NEEDLES

Embroidery size 9

Embroidery size 10

OTHER

- Wool fibre blue-green
- One tiny dark navy seed bead for the eye
- Anti-fray agent. See page 23
- Cotton fabric: blue or green to back the bird
- Square of white cotton fabric: 20cm (8")
- Hoop: 15cm (6")

STITCHES USED

Stitches are listed alphabetically in the stitch gallery on page 36.

Detached buttonhole stitch, long and short stitch, stem stitch, stem stitch filling and straight/stab stitch.

Chapter 3

Embroider the legs and feet

Use grey thread and make two long straight stitches alongside each other to form the leg. Form buttonhole stitch around both stitches (*detached buttonhole stitch* on page 37).

Note: Insert needle under both stitches at the same time.

Take needle to the back, near the branch; come up and form the little claws in straight stitch. Use a gentle tension for the stitches to curve around the branch. Make three stitches for each foot.

Embroider the bird

The bird is made separately, cut out and then attached onto the design. Use the template of the bird on the previous page and transfer it onto white cotton fabric. See page 10 for transfer techniques. Alternatively, order the stumpwork panel, printed in full colour, from your nearest stockist, or from my website www.dicraft.co.za by searching for stumpwork shapes. Stretch fabric in a 15cm (6") hoop.

Use yellow thread; outline yellow edge of tummy in stem stitch. Embroider the feathers with stem stitch filling; make rows of stem stitch close together. Use black thread and straight stitch to fill in detail on the head, beak and wing.

Use one strand of 91 and one strand of 521 (on the same needle) and fill in green feathers on tummy in stem stitch, as you did before. Fill in any gaps between the stitches in straight stitch.

Tear a piece of wool fibre and secure it in place with small stab stitches using 368 thread.

Hint: Trim the piece with your scissors if it is too bulky. Repeat for the tail. For the green feathers, stitch over the fibre with green thread; use long and short stitch, or make rows of stem stitch close together. Change to the black thread; make tiny straight stitches to create shadows between the feathers.

Work over the tail in blue thread as you did before. Secure wool fibre on the blue part of wing and head. Work over the wool in stem or straight stitch, leaving gaps between the rows for a feathery effect. Use your needle to gently pull some fibre out for a fluffy texture.

Use thread 96 to form white feathers as above. Change to grey thread and add a bead for the eye. Work tiny stab stitches around the bead to accentuate the eye. With same grey thread, outline bird in stem stitch. Use white blending filament and straight stitch to highlight the

eye, adding a few more stitches between the feathers.

Cut out the bird and place

Apply anti-fray around edge of the bird, cut out the bird, apply a backing, fill it and secure it exactly the same way as shown with the yellow bird in chapter 13 on page 134. Use grey thread to secure the bird with tiny stab stitches.

If necessary, use the blue thread to make a longer tail with a few straight stitches. Work along edge of the bird with a matching thread and use stem stitch to cover any details that are showing on the design.

Chapter 4

Dapple Dawn and Fig Tree Blue

Actual size of the rose and butterfly

Dapple Dawn

You will need

RIBBON

Di van Niekerk's silk ribbons

 7mm colour 143

13mm colour 122

THREAD

Use one strand of thread, unless suggested otherwise.

DMC six-strand embroidery floss

 840

642

Rajmahal Art.Silk

 841

 226

 96

 45

NEEDLES

Chenille size 16

Chenille size 18

Embroidery size 9

Embroidery size 10

Tapestry size 13

Tapestry size 18

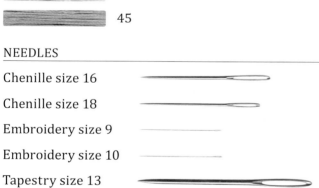

OTHER

- A piece of thin green wool for the stem (same wool used for the Sunny Roses on page 127) or use all six strands of colour 840 thread
- Fabric glue stick. Read more about this glue on page 23

STITCHES USED

Stitches are listed alphabetically in the stitch gallery on page 36.

> *Note: Read more about ribbon stitch on pages 19-20.*

Couching, French knot, pistil stitch, ribbon stitch and straight/stab stitch.

The stem

Use the piece of wool (or six strands of 840) and couch in place with one strand of matching thread. Space stitches about 1cm (⅜") apart. Cut off the excess; repeat for the other side. Place needle and thread on top of your work.

Hint: Read about working with two needles and about making holes in fabric on page 20.

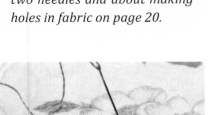

Use green 7mm ribbon and make the leaves in ribbon stitch, working from the stem outwards. Repeat for small leaves lying under the roses and for leaves on the other side.

Use green or dark grey thread and make the veins in straight stitch. At the same time, use the needle and thread to scrunch petals up slightly; make a stitch and as you insert the needle into the ribbon, move the ribbon to form a fold.

If you like, use brown thread to add a few more veins. Remember to secure and trim tails at the back, so that they don't hinder you as you work.

The roses

Use a 16 chenille needle; make a hole in your fabric. Cut a 3.5cm (1½") piece of pink ribbon and thread it onto the needle. Working from the top, insert needle into the hole, pulling gently so that most of the ribbon remains on top of your work. Remove needle at the back and leave a small tail which you should secure with white thread. Bring needle and thread to the top of your work, near centre of the rose, and place aside to use later. Trim ribbon to remove frayed ends.

Use an 18 tapestry needle and dip it into the glue stick. See page 23 for details about this glue. Roll up ribbon with sticky part of needle, using your fingers to press the edge of the ribbon against the needle. Roll until petal is short

enough for the rose. Otherwise, you could apply glue directly onto the ribbon. See the Belle Époque rose in chapter 14 on page 141.

Working quickly with needle still in the roll, and before the glue dries too much, gently secure edge of the roll with white thread and a small stab stitch. Bring needle and thread to top of your work (in the centre of the rose) and slide tapestry needle out of the roll whilst controlling the curled petal with your finger nail. Wipe your hands and needle with a damp cloth before making the next petal. Secure each petal with a tiny stab stitch.

Before making the adjoining rose, use yellow thread; make the stamens in pistil stitch, working from the centre outwards. Wrap thread three times around the needle. Fill in the green French knots with 642 and the brown knots with 841 thread, wrapping thread three times around the needle. Add a few more yellow knots, wrapping thread loosely around needle for a frilly texture.

Complete petals of the second rose and add stamens in the centre. Gently insert large tapestry needle under the petals to shape them and to lift them up and off the surface.

Fig Tree Blue

You will need

RIBBON

Di van Niekerk's organza ribbons

 25mm organza colour 89

THREAD

Use one strand of thread, unless suggested otherwise.

DMC six-strand embroidery floss

 451

453

Rajmahal Art.Silk

 25

NEEDLES

Embroidery size 9

Embroidery size 10

Notes: The wings are made separately, cut out and then attached onto the design. Use the coloured template of the butterfly; transfer it onto white cotton fabric. See page 10 for transfer techniques. Alternatively, order the stumpwork panel, printed in full colour, from your nearest stockist or from my website www.dicraft.co.za by searching for stump-work shapes. Otherwise, you could use the organza method shown for the yellow butterfly in chapter 8, page 95. You will then need the template opposite for the wings.

OTHER

- A printed butterfly on a 20cm (8") square of cotton fabric
- Temporary spray adhesive
- Anti-fray agent. See page 23
- Hoop: 15cm (6")
- Glitter glue: Bronze or brown. See page 23

STITCHES USED

Stitches are listed alphabetically in the stitch gallery on page 36.

Back stitch, French knot, pistil stitch, stem stitch and straight/stab stitch.

Template to trace

Place the printed fabric in a 15cm (6") hoop. Cut a length of the blue organza ribbon to fit over the wings and spray the ribbon with the temporary adhesive spray. Place the ribbon, sticky side down, on the printed butterfly.

Work through both layers and use black thread to make short straight or back stitches for the veins. Make the stitches alongside each other to form the broad black bands. Outline the blue edge in tiny back or stem stitches and leave the brown tips as they are.

Apply anti-fray agent to cover the entire butterfly and wait for it to dry. Cut out wings and apply glitter glue along the edges to add lustre and to cover the white bits. Set wings aside to use later.

Work on the main design; outline the body with black thread and tiny stab stitches. Make French knots for the black circular shapes, wrapping the thread three times around needle. Change to 451 thread and make the antennae in pistil stitch, wrapping thread twice around the needle. Use same thread and French knots to fill in the dark shadows on body and head.

Change to 453 thread; add more texture with French knots, working between (and on top of) the previous knots to form a rounded shape.

Use black thread to secure each wing onto the design with tiny stab stitches. Don't stitch along the outer tips; lift them up from the fabric.

> Note: It is not necessary to embroider the body as it will be worked directly onto the main design a little later.

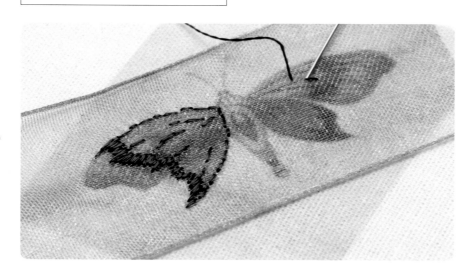

Brandy Roses and spent rose

Actual size of the roses

Brandy Roses

You will need

RIBBON

Di van Niekerk's silk ribbons

13mm colour 33

7mm colour 16

2mm colour 17

13mm colour 47 (x2)

13mm colour 46

32mm colour 47

32mm colour 46

THREAD

Use one strand of thread, unless suggested otherwise.

DMC six-strand embroidery floss

523

934

Rajmahal Art.Silk

311

226

200

45

NEEDLES

Chenille size 16

Chenille size 18

Embroidery size 9

Embroidery size 10

Tapestry size 13

Tapestry size 18

OTHER

• Fabric glue stick. Read more about this glue on page 23

STITCHES USED

Stitches are listed alphabetically in the stitch gallery on page 36.

> Note: Read more about ribbon stitch on pages 19-20.

French knot, loop stitch, ribbon stitch, running stitch, stem stitch, straight/stab stitch and twisted/twirled straight stitch.

The leaves

Thread up with green 13mm ribbon; make the leaves in ribbon stitch. Read about *making holes in fabric* on page 20 and about *securing, shaping stitches* on page 20. Use brown thread and tiny stab stitches to shape the leaf along the edge, tip and base of stitch.

Use the same thread and make the veins in straight stitch. At the same time, use needle and thread to scrunch the petals up slightly; make a stitch and as you insert the needle into the ribbon, move the ribbon to form a fold.

Change to dark green thread and make more veins alongside the brown ones to create the dark shadows. Repeat for the other six leaves.

A spent rose

Change to green 7mm ribbon; make leaves in ribbon stitch – read *about ribbon stitch* on page 19. Secure stitches with 523 thread and stab stitch. Change to grey thread; use straight stitch for veins and stem stitch for the grey stem.

Change to yellow thread; form stamens with French knots, wrapping thread three times around needle. Use brown thread and the same stitch to make the brown stamens. For the twirled stem in the next step you should make a hole in the fabric with an 18 chenille needle.

Use green 7mm ribbon; come up alongside rose. Secure tail at back of your work. Gently twist the ribbon to form a tube and insert needle into the hole that you have made.

Use 523 thread; make tiny stab stitches to secure the twisted stem, catching the side of the stem every 6mm (¼") or so. Use a gentle tension so as not to flatten stem.

Change to green 2mm ribbon; make the rounded calyx with a three-wrap French knot. Working over the calyx, form sepals in ribbon stitch. Twist ribbon once before piercing it and stitch over a 13 tapestry needle. Use 523 thread and tiny stab stitches to secure tips of the sepals, before ending off.

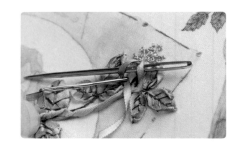

The roses

There are three Brandy Roses and it is best to start with the small rose at the back, which is made with loop and ribbon stitch. See the next step and make looped petals by stitching over a 13 tapestry needle. Make holes in your fabric as it will be easier to pull the ribbon through. Read about *making holes in fabric* on page 20 and *about ribbon stitch* on page 19.

Make the small rose
Use 13mm no. 47 ribbon; make three loops, adding a ribbon stitch on the outer edge. Use pink thread and tiny stab stitches to secure each stitch, moving stitches out of the way before making the next one. Read about *working with two needles* on page 20.

Change to 13mm 46 ribbon and make more loop stitches, securing them in place as you did before. Add some loose, puffed ribbon stitches on the outer edge of the rose.

Make a straight stitch which stretches from left to right, coming up on the left side of the rose. Pulling gently, adjust the ribbon to lie over the looped petals and insert the needle on the right-hand side. Use pink thread and tiny stab stitches to secure the stitch and end off at the back.

Make the large rose

Rolled and gathered petals are easy to make and the results are almost real. Read about *making rolled and gathered petals* on page 27. Thread up with pink thread and make a knot at the long end. Cut a 6cm (2⅜") length of 32mm no. 47 ribbon and apply glue on one corner. Read about this glue on page 23.

Use an 18 tapestry needle; roll up the sticky part of the ribbon. Use your fingers to press the edge of the ribbon against the needle and start rolling. Working quickly, while the needle is still in the roll and before the glue dries too much, secure the edge of roll with pink thread and a small stab stitch.

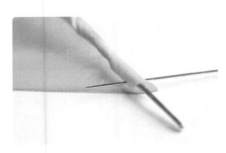

Gently slide the tapestry needle out of the roll and wipe your hands and the needle with a damp cloth. Use same thread and make small running stitches along the edge.

Glue the other corner; roll it up with the tapestry needle and catch the roll with the needle and thread. Remove the tapestry needle and wipe it with a damp cloth. Leave the thread in the needle to use in the next step.

Pull the thread to lightly gather the ribbon and insert the needle back into the first corner.

Gather it all the way to form an upright petal, which makes a perfect centre for a large rose. Leave thread on the needle as you will use it in the next step.

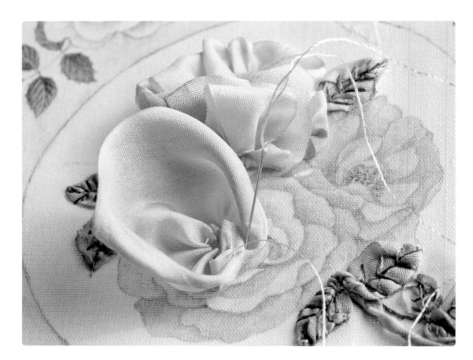

Place petal in the centre of the rose. Working on the part which is lying on the fabric, secure in place with a few stab stitches until it fits securely on the design.

Read about *making folded and gathered petals* on page 27. Cut a 9cm (3½") length of the 32mm no. 47 ribbon. Fold it in half and iron it flat with your fingertips. Cut the corners at an angle and use pink thread (with a knot at the long end) to make running stitches along the edge.

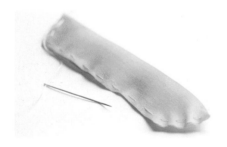

Lightly gather the ribbon; insert the needle behind the centre of the rose. As you pull thread to the back, gather some more until the piece is long enough to fit around the centre and back to where you started. Come up and catch the loose end of the petal; secure it near the starting point.

Use same thread and tiny stab stitches; secure petal around the centre of the rose. If the petal is too wide, make a stitch and as you insert the needle into the ribbon, move the ribbon to form a fold (repeating a few times) until the petal fits snugly around the centre.

Cut a 10cm (4") length of 32mm no. 46 ribbon. Fold it in half and repeat as you did before. Lightly gather the ribbon and insert the needle behind the centre of the rose.

Use tiny stab stitches to secure the petal as you did before. If it is too wide, make a stitch and as you insert the needle into the ribbon, move the ribbon to form a fold as you did before.

Hint: If you would like the centre of the rose to have more curls, insert the tapestry needle into the glue stick and roll up the edge of the ribbon some more. Use your fingers to press edge of the ribbon against the needle and start rolling. Remove needle before the glue dries and wipe your hands and the needle on a damp cloth.

Cut a 12cm (4½") length of the 32mm no. 46 ribbon. Fold it in thirds so that the top fold is about 1cm (⅜") wide. Press it flat with your fingertips.

With pink thread, use running stitches to lightly gather the ribbon along the folded edge. Insert the needle behind the centre of the rose, allowing the petal to curve into shape. Secure at the other end, close to where you started.

Catch the selvedge of the petal and stitch it onto the design – be careful not to stitch on the folded edge near the running stitches.

Gently lift and cut the gathered thread. Pull the thread out to release the folded part of the ribbon.

Gently lift the folded section to make a taller petal and use the pink thread to secure it along the base with a few stab stiches. Push parts of the petal back to the original height and make a crease below the ribbon's edge, pushing inwards gently until the folded part touches the fabric again. Use your fingertips to re-shape the rose until you are happy.

Read on page 27: *making rolled and gathered* petals. Cut a 6.5cm (2½") length of 32mm no. 46 ribbon; make a rolled and gathered petal as you did in the first step on page 73. After gathering, don't insert your needle back into the first corner like you did then – insert needle between the folds of the petals on the rose. See how the curls are facing outwards?

Fit the rose petal between the others, curving it with your fingertips. Fasten the loose edge with tiny stab stitches as you did before.

Use one strand of yellow and one strand of brown thread on the same needle; make French knots in the centre, wrapping thread three times around needle. The centre will be flattened in the very last step on the next page.

Roses in silk and organza ribbon

76

Make the medium rose

Use 13mm ribbon no. 47; make four loops 1cm (⅜") high. Secure each stitch with pink thread. Use a 12cm (4½") length of 32mm no. 46 ribbon; make a *folded and gathered petal* as you did for the large rose. Insert needle close to the looped centre and secure. Cut the thread, pull it out and lift the fold to make a taller petal. Secure as you did for the large rose.

Use a 5cm (2") piece of 32mm no. 46 ribbon; make a rolled and gathered petal as you did for the large rose. Insert petal between folds of the other petals. See how the rolls are facing inwards? Shape to form a curve; secure in place on the edge. Gently shape petal with your fingertips. To add a curl on the centre petal: insert tapestry needle into glue stick and roll up edge of the ribbon some more.

Add stamens as before. Shape and flatten centres of the roses as you form them. Add more stamens if necessary. Lift and shape the petals. Use a cotton earbud and gently curve the base of the petal to make it more bowl-shaped.

Smoky Roses and blue bow

Actual size of roses and bow

Smoky Roses

You will need

RIBBON

Di van Niekerk's silk ribbons

2mm colour 16

4mm colour 33

7mm colour 18 (x 2)

7mm colour 39 (x 2)

7mm colour 64

THREAD

Use one strand of thread, unless suggested otherwise.

DMC six-strand embroidery floss

3803

809

Rajmahal Art.Silk

226

Kreinik blending filament

032

NEEDLES

Chenille size 16

Chenille size 18

Chenille size 20

Chenille size 22

Embroidery size 9

Embroidery size 10

Tapestry size 18

OTHER

• Tiny navy seed beads for the centre of the roses

STITCHES USED

Stitches are listed alphabetically in the stitch gallery on page 36.

> Note: Read more about ribbon stitch on pages 19-20.

Back stitch, blanket stitch, French knot, ribbon stitch, stem stitch, straight/stab stitch and whipped back stitch.

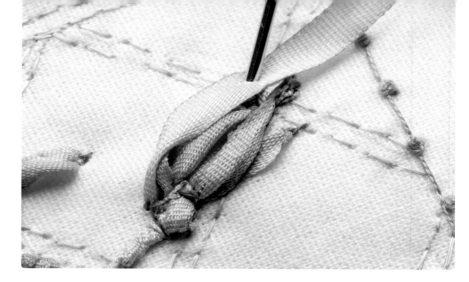

Use green 2mm ribbon; make stems with back stitches which are 4mm (⅛") long. Whip the back stitches with same ribbon, inserting needle under and over each stitch once or twice. Make the round green calyxes with two or three French knots, forming them close together, wrapping the ribbon twice around the needle. Form the sepals with green 4mm ribbon and ribbon stitch. Twist ribbon before piercing it to form curved sepals. Read *about ribbon stitch* on page 19.

Use green 7mm ribbon; make the leaves in ribbon stitch. Read about *making holes in fabric* and about *securing, shaping stitches* on page 20. Use straight stitch to form veins on the leaves with the grey and then the pink thread.

Form the rosebuds with ribbon stitch using pink 7mm ribbon. Make two or more ribbon stitches alongside or overlapping one another. Add sepals in green 4mm ribbon like you did before. Use green 4 or 7mm ribbon and cover the knots of the calyxes with ribbon stitch for a smooth surface. Use pink thread and tiny stab stitches to tuck the ribbon around the knots for a neat finish.

To make the rose showing from the back, use pink 7mm ribbon and a one-wrap French knot for each rose petal. Cover each knot with a ribbon stitch. Use pink thread and stab stitch to secure and to shape the stitches.

Change to green 7mm ribbon; make a one-wrap French knot to form the round tube of the calyx. Cover knot with ribbon stitch. Make the green sepals with ribbon stitch. Secure, shape stitches with pink thread and tiny stab stitches.

The roses are made using the same method shown for Golden Lace Roses in chapter 2 on page 54. Use pink 7mm ribbon; make a twirled ribbon rose for the centre. Secure with pink thread and French, as shown. Add a bead in the centre to create a dark shadow. Form outer rose petals in ribbon stitch and use green 4mm ribbon to make sepals as you did before.

Make the remaining roses in the same way. After forming the twirled centre, use ribbon stitch for the open roses and add a loop stitch. For closed roses: add two or three extra loops and secure them onto the twirled centre.

For larger, open roses: add loop stitches, working over a tapestry needle. Secure loops along the base (where they emerge from the fabric) with pink thread and tiny stab stitches.

To make a closed rose: gently push the loops down over the centre with your fingertips; use the pink thread and tiny stab stitches to secure the loops onto the twirled centre. Change to the shiny 032 thread and use blanket stitch on the edge of the petals to add highlights.

Make the blue bow as shown in chapter 16 on page 153. Use blue 7mm ribbon and blue thread; follow the same method.

Autumn Sunset

Actual size of the roses

Autumn Sunset

You will need

RIBBON

Di van Niekerk's silk and organza ribbons

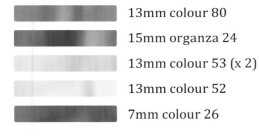

13mm colour 80

15mm organza 24

13mm colour 53 (x 2)

13mm colour 52

7mm colour 26

THREAD

Use one strand of thread, unless suggested otherwise.

Rajmahal Art.Silk

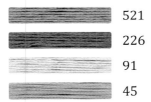

521

226

91

45

NEEDLES

Chenille size 16

Chenille size 18

Embroidery size 9

Embroidery size 10

Tapestry size 13

OTHER

- Beading wire: #0.38 in a mocha brown, purple or green
- Gold beads – tiny 15/0
- Water-soluble fabric: 20cm (8") square
- 15cm (6") hoop
- Black waterproof pigment ink pen. See page 23
- Temporary spray adhesive and anti-fray agent. See page 23

STITCHES USED

Stitches are listed alphabetically in the stitch gallery on page 36.

> *Note: Read more about ribbon stitch on pages 19-20.*

Back stitch, blanket stitch, French knot, loop stitch, overcast stitch, pistil stitch, ribbon stitch and straight/stab stitch.

The buds

Use a 15cm (6") length of 13mm no. 53 ribbon; make a pistil stitch, wrapping ribbon once around the needle.

Hint: Read about making holes in fabric on page 20. Secure tail at the back with 91 thread; come up and place needle and thread on top of your work. Read about working with two needles on page 20.

Make two ribbon stitches alongside the pistil stitch. Insert tapestry needle under the stitch and gently lift ribbon to form a soft, open stitch. Use same thread; make tiny stab stitches to secure the petals at the base and tip. When starting with a fresh ribbon, the tails should be stitched out of the way of the bud and rose. This way, there aren't too many layers to stitch through.

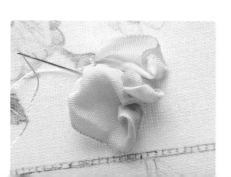

For an extra plump bud, make another petal on top. Move the yellow stitches until you can see the fabric and make a hole. Make a ribbon stitch and secure in place as before. Gently lift stitch with the tapestry needle for a rounded shape.

Use green 7mm ribbon and a straight stitch for the stem. Form the round tube with a French knot, wrapping ribbon three times around needle. Cover knot with a ribbon stitch for a smooth texture; use green thread and tiny stab stitches to tuck ribbon around the knot.

Make four of five sepals and secure with green thread.

Hint: When making a sepal on top of the bud, carefully move the yellow stitches to find a space between before making a hole in the fabric. This way, you won't stitch through the ribbon at all. Use the tapestry needle to gently lift and shape the stitches and repeat for the second bud.

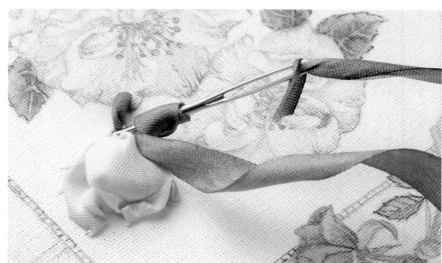

Chapter 7

The roses

Use 13mm no. 52 ribbon and start with rose in the middle. Make holes in the fabric and form the petals in ribbon stitch. Working over the tapestry needle (or your fingertip) creates softly raised petals. Use the yellow thread and small stab stitches to secure each stitch.

Make a few more petals, inserting the needle between the stitches as you did for the bud on the previous page. See how the needle has not pierced the yellow stitches? Read more *about ribbon stitch* on page 19.

Make the stitches loose and looped by working over the tapestry needle. Take care not to pull the ribbon all the way through to the back; this way, a second loop will form, which adds more texture. Secure each petal and all the loose ends at the back; trim tails of the ribbon.

Use the same ribbon and make a loop stitch in the centre, working over a tapestry needle.

Hint: If you are having difficulty in taking the needle through the fabric, use a needle gripper or small pair of pliers to grip the needle and carefully pull it through. Secure the loop and end off.

Use the 45 thread and, working from the centre outwards, make the stamens in pistil stitch, wrapping the thread twice around the needle. Make a few French knots in 45 and 521 thread and optional: add some gold beads.

Make the other roses in the same way: use ribbon stitch for the petals and add a few more stitches between the others. It is not necessary to add a loop stitch in the centre of these roses. Make the yellow and green stamens as above.

The leaves

Cut a 30cm (12") length of green 13mm silk and another of green organza ribbon. Use the temporary spray adhesive and lightly spray the organza ribbon. Place it on top of the silk ribbon to make a double layer.

Insert the water-soluble fabric in the hoop and cut off the corners so they don't get in your way as you stitch. Turn the hoop so the fabric lies flat on the tracing. See *other good tips* about using tracing paper on page 24. Use the waterproof pen and working 2cm (¾") away from the rim, trace leaves 1, 10 and 14 (opposite). These are the leaves which will have wired stems. Trace all the leaves, leaving a gap of about 2cm (¾") between for easy stitching and cutting. Number each leaf as you trace.

Cut a piece of the ribbon "sandwich" to fit under each leaf. Lightly spray the organza side of the ribbon and place it under the water-soluble fabric – the organza should face the water-soluble fabric. Work with the rim of the hoop facing up. Use green thread and whilst holding the ribbon, come up from the back in the centre of the leaf. This way, the knot won't be in the way when you cut it out later. Form the veins in tiny back stitches and work along the edge of the leaf in the same stitch.

Use grey thread and add a few more veins in back stitch. Form blanket stitch along the edge of the leaf. The stitches are spaced about 2mm (¹⁄₁₆") apart and are slanted towards the base of the leaf. End off by running the needle under the centre vein at the back of the leaf.

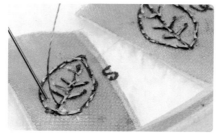

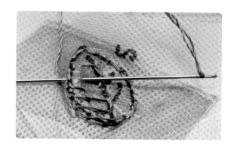

The wired stems

Cut 3 pieces of wire 6cm (2⅜") long; bend in half, using pliers to neatly flatten the fold. Start with leaf 1. Place a folded wire on the wrong side – the silky side of the ribbon. Use green thread and working on the wrong side, insert needle into the loop. Secure with a few overcast stitches, taking care to turn to the right side to check that the stitches are placed on centre vein of leaf. Secure wire with the same overcast stitches, spacing them 3mm (⅛") apart. Repeat for leaves 10 and 14.

Cut out leaf 1 and place in a bowl of water for a few minutes to dissolve the water-soluble fabric. Use a cloth to pat leaf dry and apply anti-fray agent on the entire leaf. Place the leaf on a cloth to dry. Repeat for leaf 10.

Pick up leaf 1 and refer to numbered leaves below. Gently lift yellow petal out of the way and make a hole next to the rose with the 16 chenille needle. Insert wire into the hole; secure at the back with green thread and trim with wire-cutters. Use green thread and tiny stab stitches; work along the base of the leaf to secure, allowing the tip to remain lifted off the surface of the design.

Cut out leaf 14, dip it in water, pat it dry, apply anti-fray and wait for it to dry. Secure leaf 10 followed by leaf 14.

Hint: It is easier to work with only two leaves at a time in order not to get confused with the numbers of the leaves.

Cut out the remaining leaves, noting the number alongside; place in the water, one by one. Refer to diagram opposite and to the main picture at the beginning of this chapter; secure with tiny stab stitches along the rounded base or on the side of the leaf.

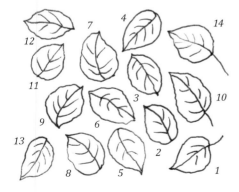

Templates to trace

Blanche Lafitte, Wisteria and Pearl Spotted Emperor

Actual size of the roses

Blanche Lafitte

You will need

RIBBON

Di van Niekerk's silk ribbons

7mm colour 33

4mm colour 99

32mm colour 115

THREAD

Use one strand of thread, unless suggested otherwise.

DMC six-strand embroidery floss

523

Rajmahal Art.Silk

200

745

NEEDLES

Chenille size 18

Chenille size 22

Embroidery size 9

Embroidery size 10

Tapestry size 18

OTHER

- Wool fibre: green
- Anti-fray agent and fabric glue stick. See page 23
- Blue water-soluble pen. See page 23
- Necklace bead: 5mm (³⁄₁₆") in any pale colour

STITCHES USED

Stitches are listed alphabetically in the stitch gallery on page 36.

Loop stitch, ribbon stitch, running stitch and straight/stab stitch.

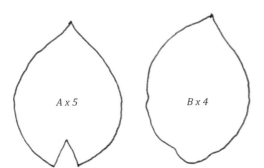

A x 5

B x 4

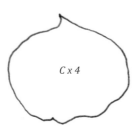

C x 4

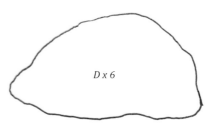

D x 6

Templates to trace

The calyx and stem

Use green thread; secure a bead to form the round tube. Thread up with green ribbon; cover bead with ribbon stitch, making another stitch or two to cover it completely. Use green thread; make tiny stab stitches to tuck the ribbon around the bead. Place needle and thread on top of your work. See *working with two needles* on page 20.

To form the stem, use green ribbon and make two straight stitches alongside each other. Whip the stitches; insert needle under and over both stitches three times to form a rounded stem. Use green thread and tiny stab stitches to secure and shape the stem. Read about *securing, shaping stitches* on page 20.

Use a fresh ribbon; make the sepals in ribbon stitch, working from the bead outwards. Read page 19: *about ribbon stitch*. To form curved sepals, twist ribbon before piercing it. Use green thread and tiny stab stitches on edge, tip and base of the sepals to secure them. To make the purple tips, use 745 thread and straight stitch.

The rose

Thin out a piece of the green wool fibre – choose a light or a dark green. A piece which is 7.5 x 5cm (3 x 2") is a good size as you don't want the centre to be too large. Fold fibre in half; twist as you would wrap a sweet. Use green thread and, after inserting it into the woollen base, wrap thread several times around the base to secure, and end off.

Use yellow ribbon and come up through the base of the ball. Make loop stitches to form yellow stamens. Using a gentle tension, make loose-fitting loops and exit through the base. Use green thread and stab stitches to secure the tails of the ribbon.

Refer to *making loose, flat petals* on page 25; make these petals in the same way. The petal templates are on page 89. Trace five A, four B and C petals and six D petals onto the 32mm pink ribbon. Cut them out, place in water, allow time to dry and apply anti-fray on the entire petal. Allow time to dry.

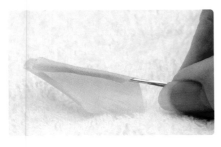

Read about *making curled petals* on page 26. Start with an A petal. Use an 18 tapestry needle; dip it into the glue stick. Use sticky part of needle to roll up edge. Press the edge of ribbon against needle; start rolling until the petal is curled. Remove needle, wipe it with damp cloth. Repeat for opposite edge.

Roll sharp end of the petal; remove needle and wipe your hands and the needle. Do this for one or two A petals, leaving the others with a sharp point. Thread up with pink thread; make a knot at the long end. Wrap petal around the green centre and use small running stitches to secure it along the base of the petal.

Wrap the thread around the ball and make a few stab stitches through the fibre and the petal. Leave thread on the needle as you will use it to secure more petals in the next step.

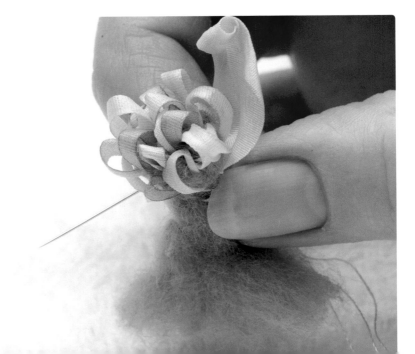

Roll up the edge of a B petal, al-lowing it to overlap the first petal. Secure with stab stitches, working through the wool fibre. Remember to wipe needle and hands every time. Use an A petal and repeat as you did in the first step. Place it to overlap the B petal and secure.

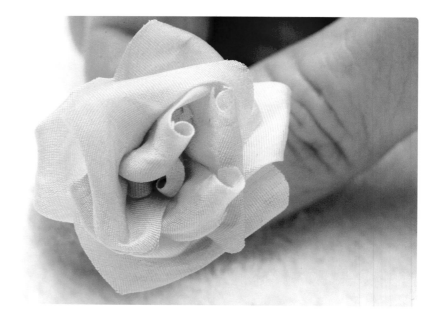

Roll up the tip and side of a B petal and secure in place. See how the petals overlap each other? By rolling petals in different ways, the rose will begin to look almost lifelike. It does not matter if rolled edges are not all the same – nature is very forgiving. Only once the rose is completed, should you judge whether you are happy with the shape or not.

Make all the A and B petals; add them to the rose. Lift the petals high, so they are taller than the centre. See how some petals curl inward and some curl outward? Roll C petals and add them too. If necessary, use needle and glue to curl the straight edges of the petals. Trim tail of the woollen fibre and petals and place the rose on design, rotating it until you are happy with the position. Secure rose with stab stitches. As you will be lifting the rose to place petals in the next step, only stitch along the base of the rose.

Roll up one edge of a D petal and gently lift the rose to place part of the petal behind it. Secure the petal on both sides, stitching the one end onto the rose to fit near the green calyx. With a gentle tension, stitch along the edge of the petal – the part that rests on the fabric.

Add another D petal. After curling the petal, gently lift the rose to stitch it in place. Make a fold to gather the petal by using needle and thread to scrunch the petal up; make a stitch, and as you insert the needle into the ribbon, move the ribbon to form a fold.

Do the same for two other petals, curling them around the rose, allowing them to overlap one another. Use tiny stitches to shape them. To make a wide, flat petal: catch the outer edge, gently pull petal downward and stitch it onto the fabric.

Add another three or four D petals, allowing them to overlap one another. Make folds in the ribbon as you stitch. Stitch along edge of the petals so that the ends cover those on the design. Use glue and needle to curl any straight edges and trim the frayed ends.

Cut three pieces of pink 32mm ribbon, 7cm (2¾") long. Make *rolled and gathered* petals as shown on page 27. Insert petal between the outer petals (which are stitched onto the fabric) and petals on the woollen centre. Lift and support the petal; secure gathered edge resting on the fabric with tiny stab stitches.

To fill in any gaps: use 5cm (2") length of 32mm ribbon and refer to *making half-rolled petals* on page 29. Add another one or two half-rolled petals, shaping and lifting them until you are happy with the rose.

Wisteria and Pearl Spotted Emperor

You will need

RIBBON

Di van Niekerk's silk and organza ribbons

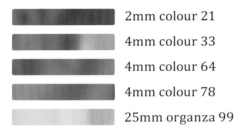

2mm colour 21

4mm colour 33

4mm colour 64

4mm colour 78

25mm organza 99

THREAD

Use one strand of thread, unless suggested otherwise.

DMC six-strand embroidery floss

809

840

452

Rajmahal Art.Silk

104

841

226

NEEDLES

Chenille size 20

Chenille size 22

Embroidery size 9

Embroidery size 10

Tapestry size 18

OTHER

- Water-soluble fabric: 20cm (8") square (x 2) 15cm (6") hoop
- Black waterproof pigment ink pen. See page 23
- Small brown seed beads: size 15/0

STITCHES USED

Stitches are listed alphabetically in the stitch gallery on page 36.

> *Note: Read more about ribbon stitch on pages 19-20.*

Back stitch, blanket stitch, French knot, pistil stitch and straight/stab stitch.

Template to trace

Wisteria

Refer to chapter 3 on page 59 and make the Wisteria using the same method. Stitch the stems first, followed by the leaves and the flowers.

Pearl Spotted Emperor

There are three Pearl Spotted Emperors in this sampler and all are made in the same way. Fill in the body with 452 thread; make French knots close together, wrapping thread twice around needle. Form the antennae in pistil stitch, wrapping thread twice around the needle. Use 104 thread; make French knots at the tips of the antennae and form the stripes on the body with straight stitches.

Place a 20cm (8") length of the yellow organza ribbon between two layers of water-soluble fabric and insert in a 15cm (6") hoop. Cut the corners so they won't get in your way.

The wing templates are on the previous page. See *other good tips* on page 24. Turn the hoop so that the fabric lies flat on the tracing and trace the wings onto the water-soluble fabric.

Use thread 104; make a knot at the long end. Come up on the outside of the wing and make a stitch to reach the centre vein. Working through all the layers, make three back stitches, one on top of another, to secure the thread. Fill in the vein in back stitch and use blanket stitch to form the wing tips. End off by running the needle under stitches at the back.

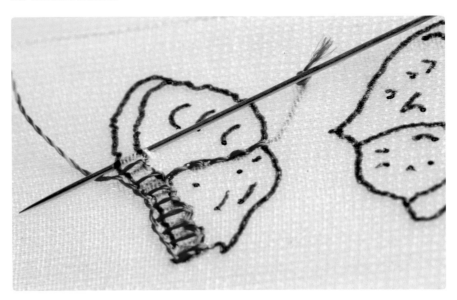

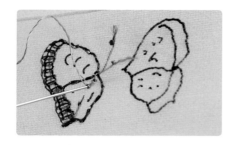  

Use 841 thread; add three seed beads on each wing. Make French knots, wrapping thread once around needle. Add small stab stitches to create texture on the wings. End off by running thread under stitches at the back.

Cut out the wings and place in a bowl of water for a few minutes to dissolve the water-soluble fabric. Place on a towel and gently pat them dry.

Whilst still damp, secure the wing onto the design with 841 thread. Use tiny stab stitches where the wing meets the body and stitch through all the layers. Use the same thread and stitch to catch the top and bottom edge of the wings, tucking them in so that the free edge lifts up for a natural finish.

Pearl Spotted Emperor near the Blanche Lafitte Rose

Pearl Spotted Emperor near the rose hips

Chapter 9

Remember Me

Actual size of the roses

Remember Me

You will need

RIBBON

Di van Niekerk's silk ribbons

 7mm colour 33

 13mm colour 37

 32mm colour 37

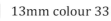 13mm colour 33

THREAD

Use one strand of thread, unless suggested otherwise.

DMC six-strand embroidery floss

 523

Rajmahal Art.Silk

 742

 745

NEEDLES

Chenille size 16

Chenille size 18

Embroidery size 9

Embroidery size 10

Tapestry size 18

OTHER

- Stem of an imitation flower for the small rose or use green ribbon and whipped back stitch
- Anti-fray agent and fabric glue stick. See page 23
- Blue water-soluble pen. See page 23
- Necklace: bead 5mm ($^{3}/_{16}$") in any pale colour

STITCHES USED

Stitches are listed alphabetically in the stitch gallery on page 36.

> Note: Read more about ribbon stitch on pages 19-20.

Back stitch, couching, detached buttonhole stitch, folded ribbon rose, ribbon stitch, running stitch, straight/stab stitch and whipped back stitch.

Template to trace

The stem and calyx

Use a stem of an imitation flower for the small rose. Bend it in shape; use wire-cutters or nail clippers; cut a piece to fit. Use green thread; couch stem in place, spacing stitches 7mm (¼") apart. Make a double stitch; end off at the back.

Come up from the back with 7mm green ribbon and wrap the stem; insert needle under and over it, working between the couching stitches with an even tension. Keep ribbon as flat as possible for a neat finish; use your fingers to hold the loop whilst wrapping the stem. With green thread and tiny stab stitches, stitch along the edge of the stem to shape any wraps that are not even.

For the short stem: make two straight stitches alongside each other. Come up at the end of the stem and whip the stitches by inserting the needle under and over both the stitches at the same time. Work back again, wrapping the stitches a second time. End off at the back.

Form the sepals in ribbon stitch. Read *about ribbon stitch* on page 19. To make curved sepals, twist the ribbon before piercing it. Use green thread and tiny stab stitches to secure the sepals. Read about *securing, shaping stitches* and about *working with two needles* on page 20.

Use the 745 thread; form the dark shadows. Use detached buttonhole stitches for large purple shadows between the sepals; wrap buttonhole stitches around a straight stitch. Form the thin ends of the sepals and the shadows alongside the stem with straight or back stitch.

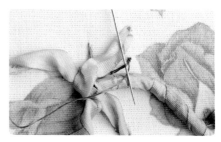

Use a necklace bead and form the round tube of large rose. Use green 13mm ribbon; cut a piece which is long enough to be tucked around the bead. Make tiny stab stitches with green thread and secure the ribbon around the bead. Add another layer on top. Otherwise, you could use green 13mm ribbon and cover bead with ribbon stitch – see the rose hips on page 105.

The roses

Make the small rose

Make a rolled-up petal: use 4cm (1⁹⁄₁₆") piece of pink 13mm ribbon and follow method used for the Dapple Dawn petals on page 65. Use 742 thread; secure curled edge with a stab stitch.

Cut another 4cm (1⁹⁄₁₆") length and make a second petal alongside, allowing it to overlap the first. Roll the end and secure as you did before.

Use 15cm (6") length of pink 32mm ribbon; fold it in half along the length. Use 742 thread and follow the method *Folded ribbon rose centre* on page 31. Leave thread in the needle to use in the next step. Trim tails of the rose for a neat edge.

Place the folded rose on top of the two petals; use tiny stab stitches to secure it in place. With a gentle tension, so as not to flatten the rose, stitch along the base of the folded rose.

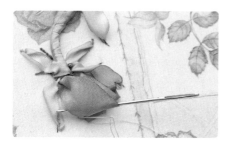

Cut another 4cm (1⁹⁄₁₆") length of ribbon; make a hole in the fabric close to folded rose. Read about *making holes in fabric* on page 20. Make a rolled-up petal, as you did in the first step and secure the base of the stitch – the curled edge remains loose at this stage. See how the curls face outwards?

Working close to the base of the rose, make a hole in your fabric and form another petal alongside, allowing it to overlap for a realistic effect. Use tiny stab stitches along the base of the petal. Gently shape the petals and use tiny stitches to secure the petals along the edges to keep their shape.

Make the large rose

Use an 18cm (7") length of 32mm ribbon and make a folded ribbon rose as you did before. End off and trim the tails for a neat edge.

Read page 25: *making loose, flat petals*. Make three petals from the petal template provided on page 98. Dip tapestry needle into glue stick; gently curl the edge of each petal. Remove the needle before the glue dries; wipe the needle and your hands on a damp cloth. Use 742 thread, make a knot at the long end and work small running stitches along the bottom edge.

If necessary, add another petal, until you are happy with the rose. Use 745 thread and one-wrap French knots (or stab stitches) to add more purple shadows.

Cut a 3cm (1³⁄₁₆") piece of green 13mm ribbon and use green thread. Make a loose sepal as shown for the Rose Gaujard in chapter 2 on page 49. Secure gathered end above the bead and stitch through the tip of the sepal, working through all the layers. Use 745 thread; add more dark shadows in straight stitch or two-wrap French knots.

Leave thread on needle and fold petal around the rose. Secure the petal onto the base with tiny stab stitches. Repeat with remaining two petals, allowing them to over-lap one another, and end off.

Position rose on design and use stab stitches to secure it along the base. Shape petals with your fingertips and press some curled edges flat between your finger-tips. Trim frayed edges. Lift last petal by gently pulling edge up-wards and outwards. To form a larger rose, make a second half-rolled petal, lift the rose and fold it around the shape. Secure, shape and lift as you did before.

Cut 7cm (2¾") length of 32mm ribbon and use 742 thread with a knot at the long end. Read page 29: *making half-rolled petals*. Leave the thread on the needle to use in the next step.

Gently fold petal around the rose (with the petal's curl facing out-wards) and allow the ends to over-lap at the starting point. Secure them with tiny stab stitches, working through the base of the rose.

Roses in silk and organza ribbon

102

Chapter 10

Rose hips and Pearl Spotted Emperor

Actual size of the rose hips and butterfly

Rose hips

You will need

RIBBON

Di van Niekerk's silk ribbons

 2mm colour 102

 13mm colour 102

 7mm colour 142

THREAD

Use one strand of thread, unless suggested otherwise.

DMC six-strand embroidery floss

 642

Rajmahal Art.Silk

 200

 745

NEEDLES

Chenille size 16

Chenille size 18

Chenille size 20

Embroidery size 9

Embroidery size 10

Tapestry size 18

OTHER
• Beads: 8mm ($^5/_{16}$") oval x 3

STITCHES USED

Stitches are listed alphabetically in the stitch gallery on page 36.

> *Note: Read more about ribbon stitch on pages 19-20.*

Back stitch, French knot, ribbon stitch, straight/ stab stitch and whipped back stitch.

The stems

Make the stems in whipped back stitch. Use pink 2mm ribbon; make stitches 3mm (⅛") in length. Take needle to the back; come up at the end of the stem and whip each stitch, inserting needle under and over the stitches. Use an even tension; hold ribbon whilst wrapping stitches so that it remains flat.

Use pink thread and secure a bead for each rose hip. Use three stitches per bead so that it fits snugly on design. End off at the back.

Rose hips

About covering a bead

There are two methods to use when covering a bead. The bead on the right was covered with the 13mm ribbon. Refer to chapter 2, Rose Gaujard, on page 49; learn how to cover a bead and how to tuck ribbon around the bead with stab stitches. For these rose hips, I will show how to use ribbon stitch to cover a bead.

Make a hole in the fabric at the base and the tip of bead with the 16 chenille needle. Read about *making holes in fabric* and about *working with two needles* (one for the thread and one for the ribbon) on page 20. Use pink 13mm ribbon; come up at base of the bead.

Make a ribbon stitch, placing the needle at an angle so the ribbon tucks itself around the bead. Use pink thread to shape ribbon with tiny stab stitches. Work along the base, edge and tip of the bead with a gentle tension.

Make a hole in the fabric and form another ribbon stitch, overlapping the previous one. Use pink thread and stab stitches to shape the ribbon and end off at the back. Start with a fresh ribbon and cover the other beads in the same way.

Use green 7mm ribbon; make leaves in ribbon stitch. Refer to Dapple Dawn leaves on page 65: make them in the same way. Use green thread to shape leaves with tiny stab stitches. Form veins on the leaves in straight stitch. Change to 745 thread; make leaf stalks in back stitch, adding more veins in straight stitch.

With two strands of green thread, make French knots on the tip of the bead, wrapping the thread once around the needle. Make green tendrils in straight or pistil stitch, working over a tapestry needle to form loose and looped stitches.

With purple thread, make dark shadows alongside the stem and hips. Use back or straight stitch (or French knots) to create the shadows.

The Pearl Spotted Emperor is made by using the same method shown in chapter 8 on page 95.

Königin von Dänemark and Golden Breasted Bunting

Actual size of roses and bird

Königin von Dänemark

You will need

RIBBON

Di van Niekerk's silk ribbons

 13mm colour 142

 7mm colour 142

 32mm colour 114

13mm colour 122

THREAD

Use one strand of thread, unless suggested otherwise.

DMC six-strand embroidery floss

 523

642

Rajmahal Art.Silk

 745

 200

NEEDLES

Chenille size 16

Chenille size 18

Embroidery size 9

Embroidery size 10

Tapestry size 18

OTHER

- 2 branched stems from an imitation flower – one thicker than the other
- Beading wire: #0.38 in a mocha brown, purple or green
- Water-soluble fabric: 20cm (8") square blocks (x 2)
- 15cm (6") hoop
- Black waterproof pigment ink pen and blue water-soluble pen. See page 23
- Temporary spray adhesive and anti-fray agent. See page 23
- Fabric glue stick. See page 23
- 4mm (⅛") seed bead – white or any pale colour

STITCHES USED

Stitches are listed alphabetically in the stitch gallery on page 36.

> Note: Read more about ribbon stitch on pages 19-20.

Back stitch, blanket stitch, couching, folded ribbon rose, ribbon stitch, running stitch and straight/stab stitch.

The stems and leaves

Use a branched stem of an imitation flower; couch the main stem with 523 thread as shown with the Remember Me Rose on page 99.

> Note: Do not couch the side stem – it will be wrapped in the next step. Use 7mm green ribbon; whip the couched stem; insert needle under and over the stem. Take needle to the back and allow the ribbon to unwind.

Come up at base of the side stem; wrap ribbon around the stem. Once you reach the tip, wrap downward again; insert needle close to main stem and pull the stems closer together. Use 523 thread; couch the stem, working over the ribbon to position it.

Repeat for the second branched stem, couching and wrapping the main stem as you did above. Wrap side stem in the same way and couch in place with green thread. Make the sepals in ribbon stitch – there is one sepal for each rose. Read more *about ribbon stitch* on page 19.

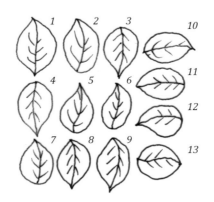

Templates to trace

Read *other good tips* on page 24 about tracing paper. Use the waterproof pen; trace outline of the hoop onto the water-soluble fabric. Working 2cm (¾") away from the edge of the circle, trace the leaves from template below, leaving a 2.5cm (1") gap between for easy stitching. Number each leaf as you trace.

Use green 13mm ribbon and cut a 2.5cm (1") strip for each leaf. Try to cut so that there is a little green and a little plum on the ribbon. The ribbon will be placed so that the plum section lies over the tip of the leaf in the next step.

Use an old towel and spray each piece with temporary spray adhesive. Place a ribbon piece on top of each leaf, sticky side down. Position so that plum section lies over tip of the leaf. Place another layer of water-soluble on top of leaves; insert all layers in a 15cm (6") hoop, stretch and tighten. Cut the corners so they don't get in your way whilst you stitch.

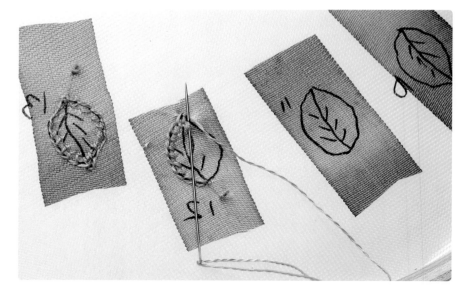

Turn the hoop so veins of the leaves are visible. The numbers are reversed, but they will guide you later. Use 642 thread and make a knot at the long end. Come up away from edge and start at base of the leaf. Make a few back stitches to secure thread and form blanket stitches along edge. Space stitches about 2mm (¹⁄₁₆") apart. The stitches should face toward the veins of the leaf.

At the tip of leaf, take the needle to the back; come up again inside the loop and complete other side of leaf. Every now and then, allow needle to hang off the back of your work for coiled thread to unwind itself.

End off with a few back stitches or by running the needle under stitches at the back. Repeat for all the leaves. Use the 745 thread; make the veins in back stitch.

Leaves number 1 and 9 are on a wired stem. Cut 7cm (2¾") piece of wire; fold over one end to form a 6mm (¼") loop. Press loop into shape with pliers or tweezers. Couch looped wire on the back of leaf 1 with 745 thread. Work down the centre vein and end off. Repeat for leaf 9. Place the hoop aside to use later.

The roses

The rose on the left

Use 30cm (12") length of pink 13mm ribbon; make a 1cm (⅜") fold and secure it along the bottom edge with pale pink thread. Make more folds, one on top of another, using the length of ribbon, securing the folds along the bottom edge. Leave thread on needle; set aside to use later.

Refer to page 25: *making loose, flat petals.* Make six A, seven B and three C petals from the templates opposite – a total of 16 petals. Place them in groups on a marked piece of paper.

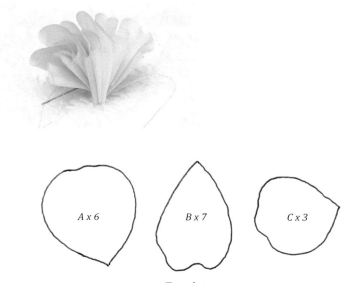

A x 6   *B x 7*   *C x 3*

Templates to trace

Use the pink thread and secure two A petals with small stab stitches, allowing the petals to overlap one another. Use three or four stitches per petal and scrunch the petals up slightly. Make a small stitch, and as you insert the needle into the ribbon, move the ribbon to form a small fold in the petal. Apply glue to tapestry needle (see *making curled petals* on page 26) and curl the edges. Wipe needle and hands with a damp cloth.

Add a B petal on the left side and curl the end. Add another on the right and do the same. See how the petal is curled twice to form an extra fold and how all the curls face towards you?

Add another B petal on the left and curl it twice to form a sharp point. Remember to wipe your needle and your hands every time you curl the edges.

Add another B petal on top and another on the right. Repeat one more time, placing petals on the left and the right, so that they overlap each other. There are now 9 petals in total. Curl the ends, making double folds for some, single folds for others.

Place folded centre on the petals, turning it so the raw ends are at the back. Use pink thread to secure it, stitching along the base (bottom edge) of the folded centre. Use a gentle tension so as not to flatten the folds.

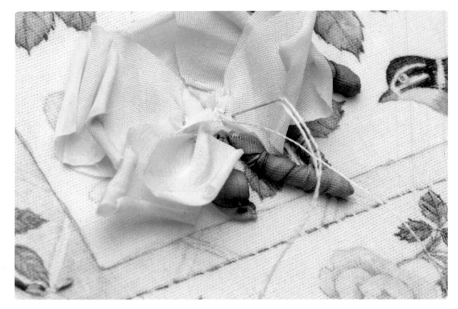

Use three C petals and secure them in front of the centre, allowing them to overlap one another. Scrunch the petals up slightly; make a stitch, and as you insert the needle into the ribbon, move the ribbon to form a fold.

Lift petals up with stitches which are placed behind the petals. Use a gentle tension and support the base of the petal with your finger-tip whilst stitching through all the layers.

Apply glue to the tapestry needle and curl the edge of the petals. Allow some curls to face towards the centre of the rose and others to face outwards.

Place four more A petals, allowing them to overlap one another. Secure in place as you did before. Curl the ends, making double curls for some, single curls for others.

Cut a 5cm (2") length of 32mm ribbon and refer to page 29: *making half-rolled petals*. Use pink thread and make a knot at the long end. Insert needle into rolled end of the petal – the pointed end.

Lift A petals up gently; secure the pointed end between the petals with a few stab stitches. Apply glue to tapestry needle; roll up the flat side to form a curled edge.

With pink thread and tiny stab stitches, secure the petal, creating folds as you stitch. Work through all the layers with a gentle tension. Use tiny stitches to secure the loose selvedge of the ribbon which is lying against the petals.

Make another half-rolled petal, using a 5cm (2") length as you did before. Secure sharp point close to the one you have just made. Make folds on the loose end and place this petal so that it overlaps the previous one. Secure with stab stitches, as you did before. Run point of the tapestry needle across the petal to form the creases.

Make and add another petal, securing below or above the others. Use tiny stab stitches to secure. Shape petals with your fingertips and make creases with point of tapestry needle.

Use 5cm (2") length of ribbon and follow *making rolled and gathered petals* on page 27. Insert the petal above others on the left side of the rose. Use tiny stab stitches to coax petal into shape. With tapestry needle and glue, make another curl or two on the edge. For a lacy finish, use sharp scissors to trim the edges of the gathered centre.

The rose on the right

This rose is made in the same way, but the centre is slightly different. Use 30cm (12") length of 13mm pink ribbon; make a *folded ribbon rose centre* (see page 31). Make the centre as shown but leave a 10cm (4") tail – don't roll it to the end. Make running stitches on bottom edge of this tail; pull thread gently to gather and fold the gathered ribbon around the rose. Stitch in place along the base. Leave needle on the thread and set aside to use later.

See templates below and prepare *loose, flat petals* as before: three A petals and six B petals. Place, secure and curl three A petals as you did for the first rose. Place folded rose centre on top, turning it so the raw end is at the back. Secure in place along the base with tiny stab stitches.

A x 3

B x 6

Templates to trace

Use six B petals and curl each one twice with tapestry needle. Secure in place with petals overlapping one another and form folds in the petals as you stitch.

Cut a 6cm (2⅜") piece of 32mm ribbon; make a half-rolled petal, as you did for the first rose. Secure in place. Make a second half-rolled petal; place so that it overlaps the first. With a gentle tension, secure petals and form creases with point of tapestry needle.

Cut a 6cm (2⅜") length; make a *rolled and gathered petal* – see page 27. Place between petals on the right and stitch in place. Gently lift the petals and shape with your fingertips, pulling the edge downward for a realistic effect. Use stab stitches to shape the petals so that they fit around the centre of the rose.

The bud

Cut a 6cm (2⅜") piece of 13mm ribbon; thread it onto the needle. From the top of your work, insert needle into the fabric. Pull gently to the back, leaving a 3cm (1³⁄₁₆") piece on top. Remove needle at the back; secure tail with pink thread. Dip tapestry needle into the glue stick and roll ribbon to form the bud. Secure it with pink thread and tiny stab stitches.

Attach a bead for the round tube. Cover it with 7mm green ribbon and use one or two straight stitches. With 745 thread and tiny stab stitches, tuck the ribbon around the bead.

Make the sepals in ribbon stitch. Work over the tapestry needle for soft, open stitches. Use 745 thread to secure the tip of bud and the sepals with a few stab stitches – this will also create the purple shadows on the bud.

The leaves

Refer to the numbers on the wrong side of the hoop and cut out the leaves. Place, one by one, memorising the number, into a bowl of water to dissolve the water-soluble fabric. Remove after a few minutes, pat dry with a cloth and place on a piece of paper which is numbered according to the leaf. Repeat for every leaf.

Refer to numbered leaves on the template opposite. Use green thread and tiny stab stitches to secure each leaf, leaving wired leaves till last. Where the leaf fits under the rose petals, gently lift them up before securing the leaf. Stitch along the base of the leaf and, if you find that the leaf is too loose on the design, secure the tip of the leaf as well.

Add the wired leaves last, as follows: pick up leaf 1, make a hole near the stem with 16 chenille needle. Insert wire into the hole, secure at the back with green thread. Trim the tail with wire-cutters. Stitch along base of every leaf, stitching over the wire to secure it.

Hint: If the petals on the design are still visible, gently position the ribbon petals; use pink thread and tiny stab stitches to secure the petal's edge onto the fabric.

Golden Breasted Bunting

You will need

THREAD

Use one strand of thread, unless suggested otherwise.

Rajmahal Art.Silk

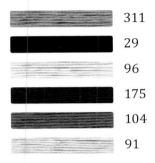

311
29
96
175
104
91

NEEDLES

Embroidery size 9

Embroidery size 10

Did you know? *Golden Breasted Buntings are found in wooded forests in Southern Africa where they forage for food on the ground. It's a shy bird and is often seen in small groups, in pairs, or on its own. It's monogamous and breeds with one partner for life. Known in Afrikaans as Rooirugstreepkoppie.*

OTHER
- Wool fibre: yellow
- Wool fibre: brown
- Fabric glue stick. Read more about this glue on page 23
- Anti-fray agent. See page 23
- Cotton fabric: blue or green to back the bird
- Square of white cotton fabric: 20cm (8")
- Hoop: 15cm (6")

STITCHES USED

Stitches are listed alphabetically in the stitch gallery on page 36.

Detached buttonhole stitch, French knot, long and short stitch, running stitch and straight/ stab stitch.

Make the bird's legs in detached buttonhole stitch. Use 311 thread and refer to the Blue Tit in chapter 3 on page 61 – the legs and feet are made in the same way.

The bird is made separately, cut out and attached onto the design. Use the template of the bird below and transfer it onto white cotton fabric. See page 10 for transfer techniques. Otherwise, you are welcome to order the stumpwork panel, printed in full colour, from your nearest stockist, or from my website www.dicraft.co.za by searching for stumpwork shapes. Stretch the fabric in a 15cm (6") hoop.

Place the yellow wool fibre on top of bird and thin it out a bit. Use 311 thread; make tiny running stitches along the edge of the bird to secure the fibre. Turn the hoop over to check that you are stitching along the edge.

Use the same thread; secure brown fibre in the same way. Change to 29 thread; use point of needle to open area around the eye and outline it in stab stitch. Make a French knot for the eye, wrapping thread once around needle. Fill in black head feathers with long and short stitch. Use straight stitch to form black detail on beak, wing and tail.

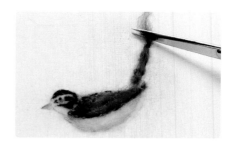

Change to 96 thread and then to 175 thread and do the same. Change to 104 and then 91 thread; use long and short stitch for the feathers on the tummy. Apply anti-fray along edge of the bird, cut it out, apply a backing, fill it and secure with the 311 thread; exactly the same way as shown with the yellow bird in chapter 13 on page 134.

Spider web, Dusky Maiden and Purple Emperors

Actual size of the roses, spider web and butterfly

Spider web

You will need

THREAD

Use one strand of thread, unless suggested otherwise.

Rajmahal Art.Silk

 226

NEEDLES

Chenille size 18

Embroidery size 10

OTHER

• A spider earring, made from sterling silver, available from jewellery stores or flea markets. Or you could email me: di@dicraft.co.za and I will arrange to get one for you.

STITCHES USED

Stitches are listed alphabetically in the stitch gallery on page 36.

Back stitch, split stitch and straight/stab stitch.

The web

Use grey thread; make the circular spirals of the web in stem or split stitch. Keep stitches short, about 3mm (⅛") long, for a neat outline.

Form the long radials of the spider web in back stitch, making one stitch between each circular spiral.

The spider

A spider earring is perfect for a web. Use a pair of pliers to bend shaft backwards. Make a hole in fabric with 18 chenille needle; insert the spider into the hole. Secure bent shaft at the back with tiny stitches.

Did you know? *Spider webs have been in existence for at least 140 million years and the intricate webs are made from spider silk – a protein fibre.*

Roses in silk and organza ribbon

Dusky Maiden

You will need

RIBBON

Di van Niekerk's silk ribbons

 7mm colour 16

 13mm colour 58

 7mm colour 60

THREAD

Use one strand of thread, unless suggested otherwise.

DMC six-strand embroidery floss

 523

Rajmahal Art.Silk

 745

226

253

45

841

175

NEEDLES

Chenille size 16

Chenille size 18

Embroidery size 9

Embroidery size 10

Tapestry size 18

OTHER

• Fabric glue stick. See page 23

STITCHES USED

Stitches are listed alphabetically in the stitch gallery on page 36.

> Note: Read more about ribbon stitch on pages 19-20.

French knot, ribbon stitch, split stitch, straight/stab stitch and twirled ribbon rose.

Did you know? *The genus Rosa has some 150 species and has been around for 35 million years. Probably the most admired flower in the world, fragrant rose petals have been used for centuries to make aromatic oils.*

The leaves, sepals and stem

See page 19 for more *about ribbon stitch*. Use green 7mm ribbon; make leaves and sepals in ribbon stitch. Read about *securing, shaping stitches* on page 20. Use 745 thread to secure and to shape the stitches. Make veins on leaves in straight stitch. Use two strands of grey thread; make the stem in split stitch. Make two rows close together to form a thick stem.

The rose

Use red 13mm ribbon and, working from the centre outwards, make the first layer of petals in ribbon stitch.

Hint: Read about making holes in fabric on page 20.

Use two strands of 45 thread; make yellow stamens with French knots, wrapping thread twice around needle. Change to one strand of light brown thread; add more stamens in the same way. Use dark brown thread; make three knots in the very centre.

Use 7mm red ribbon and red thread; make the small bud with a twirled ribbon rose. See page 33: *twirled ribbon rose*. Change to 7mm green ribbon; make the round tube of the calyx with a French knot, wrapping ribbon twice around needle.

Insert a tapestry needle into the loop that forms when you take ribbon to the back. This will help to create a petal with a curled up tip. Pull ribbon gently to lock the ribbon around needle. Read about *working with two needles* on page 20. Use red thread to secure the petals on the tip and the base of every stitch. Repeat for the second rose.

Use the same ribbon and cover the knot with a straight stitch, making a second stitch on top if necessary. Use green thread and tiny stab stitches to shape the ribbon around the knot.

Make the sepal in ribbon stitch, twisting the ribbon once or twice before piercing it for an interesting effect. Read more *about ribbon stitch* on page 19.

Make a second sepal on the other side, twisting the ribbon as before. Add a third sepal on top using the same stitch. Use green thread and tiny stab stitches to secure and shape the stitches.

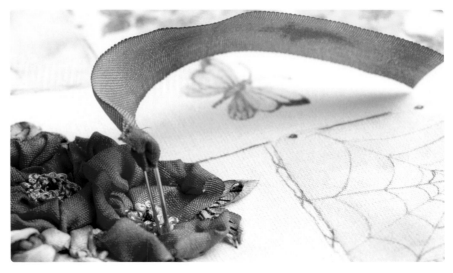

Cut a 5cm (2") length of 13mm ribbon and read about *making holes in fabric* on page 20. Insert needle from the top of your work, inserting it near the centre of the rose, working between the ribbon stitches. Pull gently so that most of the ribbon remains on top of your work. Remove needle at the back and leave a tail which you should secure with the red thread.

Bring needle and thread to the top of your work, near the centre of the rose. Stitch along the base of the petal with tiny stab stitches. Trim ribbon to remove any frayed ends. Add a second petal, stitching along the base as you did before.

Apply glue on the end of the ribbon. Use an 18 tapestry needle and, after dipping it into the glue stick, roll up the ribbon with sticky part of the needle. Use your fingers to press edge of the ribbon against the needle and start rolling.

Roll until the petal is short enough for the rose. See how the petal curls towards the yellow centre? Repeat for the second petal.

Make two petals for second rose in the same way. Shape petals once again and insert tapestry needle under the ribbon stitches to lift them off the surface of the fabric.

The Purple Emperor butterflies are made using the same method as in chapter 16 on page 153.

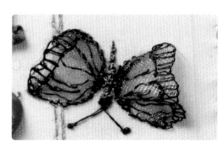

Gently bend the curled edges with your fingertips and use needle to shape the curls again if they have been pressed too flat. Use red thread and tiny stab stitches to catch the petals and secure them to rest over the centre of the rose. Use a gentle tension so the petals are not flattened – they should stand tall above the others.

Sunny Roses, bird's nest and Willow Warbler

Actual size of roses, nest and bird

Sunny Roses and bird's nest

You will need

RIBBON

Di van Niekerk's silk ribbons

	7mm colour 16
	7mm colour 15
	4mm colour 33
	7mm colour 99
	32mm colour 99

THREAD

Use one strand of thread, unless suggested otherwise.

DMC six-strand embroidery floss

	840
	523

Rajmahal Art.Silk

	226
	311
	45
	521

NEEDLES

Chenille size 16	
Chenille size 18	
Embroidery size 9	
Embroidery size 10	
Tapestry size 18	

OTHER

• A 25cm (10") piece of brown-green wool for the branches and some raffia for the bird's nest

> *Hint: If you would like to use the hand-painted raffia, as I have done, you are welcome to email me: di@dicraft.co.za and I will arrange this (and the piece of wool) for you.*

• Anti-fray agent and blue water-soluble pen. See page 23
• Oval beads (x 3): blue, white or cream for the eggs
• One or two small feathers for the nest

STITCHES USED

Stitches are listed alphabetically in the stitch gallery on page 36.

> *Note: Read more about ribbon stitch on pages 19-20.*

Back stitch, couching, detached buttonhole stitch, French knot, pistil stitch, ribbon stitch, running stitch, straight/stab stitch, twirled ribbon rose and whipped back stitch.

The stem, leaves and bird's legs

Cut 13cm (5") lengths of wool; use 840 thread and couch the wool to form stems. Place wool at beginning of the stem and stitch in place to secure it. Separate the wool to form thinner stems and secure with the same thread. Space couching stitches about 1cm (⅜") apart and use a gentle tension so as not to flatten the wool. Trim the wool at the end of stems.

Cut pieces of wool for the short and curved stems; couch in place. The raw ends lie on top of the fabric (the wool is not taken to the back) and the ends will be covered with leaves and roses a little later.

Make the thin green stem (running up to the bird) with 523 thread and whipped back stitch. Read *about ribbon stitch* on page 19. To make leaves: use 7mm ribbon no. 15 and then no. 16, alternating the colours when you thread up with a fresh piece. Make ribbon stitches, working from stem outwards, stitching over the stem when required. Make small leaves on the stem with green 4mm ribbon and the same stitch. Use 226 thread to make veins on the leaves in straight stitch.

Change to two strands of 311; make the bird's legs in straight stitch. Make a second stitch alongside. Repeat for lower part of leg. Cover the stitches with buttonhole stitch – see detached buttonhole stitch in the stitch gallery. Insert needle under and over the stitches to form a rounded shape. Repeat for other straight leg.

Make little feet in straight stitch, working over the stem. Use a gentle tension and make three stitches for each foot.

The roses

Use green 7mm ribbon no. 15 or 16; make the round tube of the calyx with a French knot, wrapping ribbon twice around needle. Use 523 thread to neaten the knot with tiny stab stitches. Place ribbon and thread on top of work to use later.

See *twirled ribbon rose* on page 33. Make small rosebuds with this stitch. You could also refer to chapter 2 on page 54 – the Golden Lace roses are made in the same way.

Insert needle into centre of bud and secure the twirls with yellow thread and tiny stab stitches or French knots. Work with a gentle tension so as not to flatten the bud. To make the large rosebud just above, form two twirled roses alongside each other.

Make the sepals in ribbon stitch using colour 15 or 16. Stitch from the round tube outwards. Work with a gentle tension and let the stitches cover part of the yellow bud. Repeat for the double bud above it; refer to main picture on page 126.

Use thread 523; secure the sepals at tip and base with tiny stab stitches. If necessary, use stab stitches along the edge of the sepal (lying against the fabric) to support the stitch. Use green

ribbon; work a straight stitch over the green knot of the calyx at the end of the stem. Shape stitch with tiny stab stitches; read more about *shaping, securing stitches* on page 20.

Use yellow 32mm ribbon and, from the templates opposite, trace 10 large circles and 2 small circles. Refer to *making loose, flat petals* on page 25 and use the same method.

Roses in silk and organza ribbon

Take a large circle and use yellow thread with a knot at the long end. Form a circle of short running stitches around the shape. The stitches should be about 3mm (⅛") in length, worked 2mm (¹⁄₁₆") away from the edge.

Pull gently to gather the thread and insert needle into centre of the bubble. Pull needle and thread through and hold thread whilst trimming the frayed edges. Be careful not to cut the thread.

Flatten the bubble by pinching it between your thumb and index finger, shaping the edge with your fingertips. Place the rose on design and secure with a stab stitch. Pull thread to tighten stitch so the rose scrunches up slightly. Repeat a few times. Catch the underside of the rose; tuck in gathered edge with a few stab stitches and come up in the centre of the rose.

Form stamens with pistil stitch, wrapping thread twice around needle. Work from the centre outwards. To scrunch the rose up: insert needle into the ribbon and pull it inwards before piercing the fabric. Take needle to the back of your work.

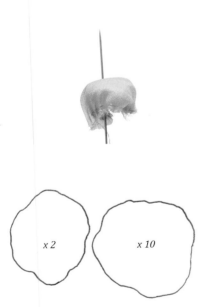

x 2   *x 10*

Templates to trace

To form a half-open rose: make stamens only on the part which rests on the fabric. Use same thread and make tiny stab stitches on the back of the rose to coax it into shape.

Repeat for the other roses. Use smaller circles for the two little roses which are amongst the cluster of roses lying below the butterfly's wing. Add brown stamens with a French knot, using 311 thread, wrapping it twice around the needle.

Form the green disc in the very centre with 521 thread, making one to three French knots close together. Shape the roses with your fingertips and lift edges up and off the design.

If the roses are a little flat, use yellow thread and come up in the centre. Make a straight stitch, piercing only the ribbon. Pull the ribbon inwards with your needle, pulling towards the centre of the rose. Pierce the fabric and take needle to the back of your work.

The nest

Use grey thread and couch a feather or two in the centre of the nest. Bring needle and thread to top of work; place aside to use in the next step.

Split a piece of raffia into thin strips which are about 10cm (4") long. Couch in place with brown thread. Space couching stitches quite far apart – stitch only where the raffia requires shaping. Twirl raffia round and round, overlapping the previous layer and using a gentle tension as you couch.

Add a second piece, and a third or fourth piece, building the nest around the feathers.

Use the same brown thread and secure a bead on the nest. Use two or three stitches to secure it in place.

Repeat for the two other beads and end off. Rethread, making a knot at the long end.

Couch more raffia pieces, as you did before, twirling them around to form the nest. Remember to use a gentle tension and to stitch only where necessary. End off at the back. Don't you think it's a cute little nest?

> *There is nothing in which the birds differ more from man than the way in which they can build and yet leave a landscape as it was before.* Robert Lynd – The Blue Lion and Other Essays

Willow Warbler

You will need

THREAD

Use one strand of thread, unless suggested otherwise.

Rajmahal Art.Silk

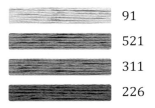

	91
	521
	311
	226

Kreinik blending filament

 032

NEEDLE

Embroidery size 10

OTHER

- Wool fibre: yellow
- Wool fibre: green
- Anti-fray agent. See page 23
- Cotton fabric: blue or green to back the bird
- Square of white cotton fabric: 20cm (8")
- Hoop: 15cm (6")

STITCHES USED

Stitches are listed alphabetically in the stitch gallery on page 36.

Back stitch, French knot, running stitch, stem stitch and straight/stab stitch.

Prepare the little bird

The bird is made separately, cut out and then attached onto the design. Use the template of the bird opposite; transfer it onto white cotton fabric. See page 10 for transfer techniques.

Alternatively, order the stumpwork panel, printed in full colour, from your nearest stockist or from my website www.dicraft.co.za by searching for stumpwork shapes. Stretch the fabric in the 15cm (6") hoop.

Use two strands of 311; fill in brown detail on the neck in straight stitch, and on wings in back stitch. Start with a knot, but come up away from edge of bird so the knot won't be in the way when you cut it out. Change to 521 thread; fill in green detail in slanted straight stitch.

Thin out a piece of yellow fibre; place it on top of the bird. Use one strand of 91 and one strand of 521 on the same needle; make slanted straight stitches to cover part of the woolly fibre, leaving gaps for a feathery texture. Turn hoop over to check that the stitches are on the edge of bird. Trim the excess fibre.

Use a piece of yellow fibre and a piece of green fibre; place alongside each other and cover the tail. Use 311 and make a few straight stitches to secure, as you did before. Trim along the edges.

Repeat and place a thin layer of yellow and green fibre on the wing. Use same thread and stitch to secure, as you did before. Add more straight stitches to form the detail on wing and neck. Fill in the outline of beak with same stitch.

Add a layer of yellow fibre on the head; secure with straight stitches along the edge. Gently move fibre to open the eye area; outline eye with tiny stab stitches. Change to grey thread; add grey wing detail with slanted straight stitches or stem stitch. Make a French knot for the eye, wrapping thread three times around the needle.

Use 032 blending filament; outline eye area again to add highlights. Repeat on wing, beak and anywhere else you would like to add a bit of sparkle. Cut out the bird, leaving a seam. Apply anti-fray agent on entire shape, allow time to dry and cut along the edge of the bird.

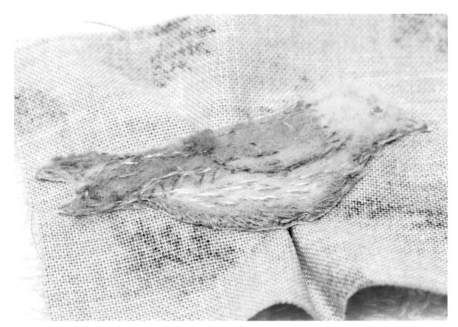

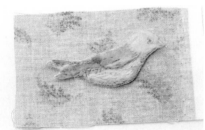

Use a piece of cotton fabric in any complementary colour – fine cotton with a high thread count is good, as it tends to fray less.

Use thread 521; make small running stitches along edge of bird, starting on the flat part above the wing. As you stitch, make a fold in the fabric which will create extra space to form a rounded shape in the next step. Work around the edge toward the starting point and leave a small gap.

Use yellow or green woolly fibre and fill the gap to make a fat little bird. Close the gap with stitches. Make a few stitches on the bird, stitching through all the layers to fasten the backing onto the bird. Use tiny stitches along the edge where the backing may have loosened.

Place bird on design; use same green thread to secure it with a few stab stitches. Use a gentle tension and space stitches quite far apart, stitching only where necessary to secure it onto the design. Allow beak, tip of wing and tail to stand free – lifted off the surface of the design.

Roses in silk and organza ribbon

Belle Époque

Actual size of rose

Belle Époque

You will need

RIBBON

Di van Niekerk's silk ribbons

 7mm colour 143

 32mm colour 86

THREAD

Use one strand of thread, unless suggested otherwise.

DMC six-strand embroidery floss

 642

Rajmahal Art.Silk

 745

91

NEEDLES

Chenille size 16

Chenille size 18

Embroidery size 9

Embroidery size 10

Tapestry size 18

OTHER

- A piece of stem from an imitation flower
- Blue water-soluble pen. See page 23
- Anti-fray agent. See page 23
- Fabric glue stick. See page 23

STITCHES USED

Stitches are listed alphabetically in the stitch gallery on page 36.

Note: Read more about ribbon stitch on pages 19-20.

Back stitch, folded ribbon rose, ribbon stitch, running stitch, straight/stab stitch and whipped back stitch.

Did you know? *To give a peach rose to someone implies feelings of respect, appreciation, gratitude, sincerity and compassion.*

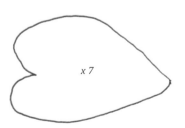

x 7

Template to trace

The shadows, stem and calyx

Start with the purple shadows and tips of the sepals. Use thread 745; make small back stitches. Whip stitches for a neat finish.

Bend the stem into shape. Use same thread and tiny stab stitches to secure it onto the design. Work along edge of the stem, catching the ribbon as you insert needle to the back. Space stitches about 1cm (⅜") apart; work both sides of stem.

Make sepals in ribbon stitch. Read pages 19 and 20: *about ribbon stitch* and *securing, shaping stitches*. For the curved petals, twist the ribbon before piercing it. Use thread 745 and tiny stab stitches to secure sepals on the tips. Use

same stitch on edge of the ribbon to shape and position the sepals so that they fit on the design.

Cut a stem of an imitation flower to fit on the design; use a pair of wire-cutters. Glue the one end. Wrap green 7mm ribbon around stem and, before you reach the other end, dip it into the glue stick. Wrap to the end, wrap downwards again to cover it a second time. Use green thread and tiny stitches to secure ribbon onto the stem.

The rose

Refer to technique: *folded ribbon rose centre* on page 31. Thread up yellow thread; make a knot at the long end. Cut a 15cm (6") length of 32mm ribbon. Make a 1cm (⅜") fold in the ribbon, ironing it flat with your fingertips. Make a folded ribbon rose as shown on page 31. Leave thread on needle and set rose aside to use later.

Read *making loose, flat petals* on page 25 – the petal template is on page 136. Trace seven petals onto the 32mm ribbon. Cut out and place in water, allow time to dry and apply anti-fray on the entire petal. Allow time to dry.

Read about *making curled petals* on page 26. Use an 18 tapestry needle; dip it into glue stick and roll up the edge. Remove needle; wipe with a damp cloth and repeat for the opposite edge. See how the petals differ? By curling the tips in different ways, the petals appear to be almost life-like.

Wrap the petal around the folded rose; use thread (which you left hanging on the rose earlier) and stitch along the base, stitching through all the layers. Leave thread on needle as you will use it again in the next step.

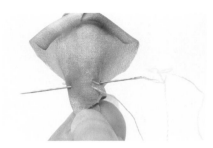

Add two more petals in the same way, allowing them to overlap one another. Stitch along the base of the petal through all the layers. Trim tails; place rose on design, rotating it until you are happy with the position.

Secure rose with a few stab stitches. As you will lift the rose to place the petals in the next step, stitch only along base of the rose, as shown in the photo above.

Place another petal near the rose. See how the curls face towards the fabric? Make a fold to gather the petal by using needle and thread to scrunch petal up slightly; make a stitch, and as you insert the needle into the ribbon, move the ribbon to form a fold. Make a few more stab stitches along the base of the petal.

Add another petal, stitching along the base as you did above. Catch the curled edge of the petal and pull it in to match the petal which is on the design. Secure the edge with a stab stitch, using a gentle tension so as not to flatten the edge.

Place another petal and repeat as you did above, creating a fold in the petal and pulling it inwards so that it fits over the petal on the design.

Place the last petal as shown, so that it overlaps the green sepals. Secure, using stab stitch to make folds in the ribbon. Stitch along the base only, as you will flip it over in the next step.

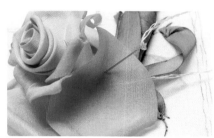

Push the petal forward; secure it onto the centre with stab stitches. Work along the base to hold it in the upright position. This will provide the space required for the large petals in the next step.

Cut 9cm (3½") length of 32mm ribbon and read page 27 *making rolled and gathered petals.* Pull thread to gather petal slightly and hold thread to retain the gathers. Place petal (with the curl facing outwards) to fit from behind the rose centre to where needle is shown below.

Use the same thread and tiny stab stitches to secure the petal around the centre of the rose. If the petal is too wide, make a stitch and as you insert the needle into the ribbon, move the ribbon to form a fold (repeating a few times) so that the petal fits snugly around the centre.

Make another 9cm (3½") petal and gather slightly as you did above. Hold the thread to retain the gathers and fold the petal in half. Use a stab stitch to join the two ends. Place the petal as shown above and insert the needle into the fabric, coming up in the fold of the petal.

Use a stab stitch to secure the fold of the petal. Go back to the starting point to add a few more stitches.

Fold the petal around the centre and hold it whilst working small stab stitches along the base. Insert needle at an angle so the stitches will support the petal against the rose centre.

Roses in silk and organza ribbon

Cut a 4cm (1¾") piece of 32mm ribbon. Use yellow thread with a knot at the long end. Make small running stitches along one raw end; gather slightly and use same thread to secure it onto the rose. End off at the back.

Roll until petal is short enough for the rose. See how the petal curls towards the stem? Cut another 4cm (1¾") piece of ribbon; repeat for a second petal.

Add a third petal and after applying the glue, roll it up as before. Add a fourth petal above the stem. Gently lift and shape the petals with your fingertips. Pinch the gathered end near the centre and scrunch the petal up a bit. Use tiny stab stitches to hold the shape.

To make more curls, dip the needle into the glue. Insert needle into the curled end, curling it a bit more. Hold ribbon with your fingernail as you slide needle out, which will form creases in the curl. Gently lift petals up off the surface with tapestry needle. Use sharp embroidery scissors to trim the frayed ends.

Hint: For a plumper rose, you could add another one or two petals, as you did before.

Apply glue on the end of the ribbon and use the 18 tapestry needle. After dipping it into the glue stick, roll up ribbon with the sticky part of the needle, using your fingers to press the edge of the ribbon against the needle.

Chapter 15

Peace Rose and Wisteria branch

Actual size of Peace Rose and Wisteria branch

Peace Rose and Wisteria branch

You will need

RIBBON

Di van Niekerk's silk ribbons

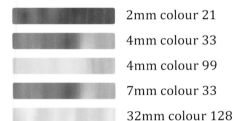

	2mm colour 21
	4mm colour 33
	4mm colour 99
	7mm colour 33
	32mm colour 128

THREAD

Use one strand of thread, unless suggested otherwise.

DMC six-strand embroidery floss

	840
	523

Rajmahal Art.Silk

	226
	200

NEEDLES

Chenille size 16

Chenille size 18

Chenille size 20

Chenille size 22

Embroidery size 9

Embroidery size 10

Tapestry size 18

OTHER

• Wool fibre: green
• Anti-fray agent and fabric glue stick. See page 23
• Blue water-soluble pen. See page 23

STITCHES USED

Stitches are listed alphabetically in the stitch gallery on page 36.

Note: Read more about ribbon stitch on pages 19-20.

Back stitch, chain stitch, French knot, loop stitch, ribbon stitch, running stitch, stem stitch, straight/stab stitch, twisted straight stitch, whipped back stitch and whipped straight stitch.

The Peace Rose

Make the stem and sepals

Thread up with green 7mm ribbon; make stem in twisted straight stitch. Use green thread and tiny stab stitches to hold the shape. Read *about ribbon stitch* on page 19; make sepals in ribbon stitch, working from the rose outwards. To form curved sepals, twist the ribbon before piercing it. Use green thread and tiny stab stitches: secure sepal on tip and base, and along the edge, if necessary.

Make the rose

The first part of this rose is prepared in the same way as the Blanche Lafitte Rose in chapter 8. More petals are added in the steps that follow, which turns it into a Peace Rose.

Refer to pages 90-93; make the Blanche Lafitte Rose using 32mm no. 128 ribbon. Make the centre with green fibre and add yellow stamens. Trace and curl the petals provided on page 89 and secure them onto the woollen centre. Prepare and place rose on design, moving it until you are happy with the position.

See page 92 and 93. Make the D petals and secure as shown. Make the rolled and gathered petals and insert them between the petals. Add one or two half-rolled petals to fill in any gaps. Lift and shape petals with your fingertips or tapestry needle. Trim any frayed edges that may be visible.

The Blanche Lafitte Rose

Make the Peace Rose by adding more petals

Shape the rose with your fingertips, turning it very gently in a clockwise direction. Adjust large petals to fit snugly around the rose. Use needles or pins to hold their position and make small stab stitches with pink thread. Stitch along the base of the petals, working through all the layers to secure the folds.

Prepare five more D petals from template on page 89. Roll and curl twice to form twirled ends. Secure as you did for Blanche Lafitte Rose. Use more stab stitches, inserting the needle into the petal, tucking it against the main part of rose. Add four more petals, working around the rose.

Cut three 7cm (2¾") lengths of 32mm ribbon. Make *rolled and gathered petals* as shown on page 27. Lift rose; insert petal between outer petals (which are lying on the design) and main part of the rose. Pull petal to fold it around the other petals and secure.

Add a second petal, starting above the sepals, curling it towards the right. Pull petal to fold it around the other petals and secure. Lift petal and use point of tapestry needle to push edge under the main part of the rose. Stitch in place.

Repeat this for the third petal, starting on the left side, curling towards the right. Secure with small stab stitches. Lift the petal and use the point of the tapestry needle to push the edge under the main part of the rose. Stitch in place.

Make two *rolled and gathered petals*, 9cm (3½") in length. Wrap the first petal around the others to fit snugly around the rose. Secure with stab stitches as you did before.

Add the second 9cm (3½") petal; start at back of the rose and repeat. With a gentle tension, lift and support the rose whilst curling the petal around it. Stitch in place. See how the petal supports the rose? Every petal which is added helps to lift the others.

Use your fingertips to shape and lift the petals to form a pleasing shape. Use stab stitches to hold the position of the petal by working through the base of the rose. Trim any frayed ends. To create a frilly texture near the stamens, cut the edge of some curled petals.

Make a 6cm (2⅜") *rolled and gathered petal*; add it on the right, between the outer petals (lying on the design) and the main part of the rose. To fill any gaps, add one or two more petals. Place them between the others. Shape and secure with stitches. Lift and shape petals with your fingertips until you are happy with your rose.

The Wisteria branch is made in the same way as the Wisteria in chapter 3. Use the brown 4mm ribbon for the branch and the green 4mm ribbon for the leaves; follow the directions on page 59.

Michaelangelo, blue bow and Purple Emperors

Actual size of the roses

Michaelangelo

You will need

RIBBON

Di van Niekerk's silk ribbons

- 2mm colour 17
- 4mm colour 17
- 7mm colour 35
- 32mm colour 99
- 13mm colour 99
- 13mm colour 53
- 13mm colour 56
- 4mm colour 54

THREAD

Use one strand of thread, unless suggested otherwise.

DMC six-strand embroidery floss

- 523

Rajmahal Art.Silk

- 226
- 45
- 311
- 91

NEEDLES

- Chenille size 16
- Chenille size 18
- Embroidery size 9
- Embroidery size 10
- Tapestry size 13
- Tapestry size 18

OTHER

- Blue water-soluble pen and fabric glue stick. See page 23
- Wool fibre: yellow

STITCHES USED

Stitches are listed alphabetically in the stitch gallery on page 36.

> Note: Read more about ribbon stitch on pages 19-20.

Back stitch, detached chain, French knot, pistil stitch, ribbon stitch, running stitch, stem stitch, straight/stab stitch, twisted straight stitch and whipped back stitch.

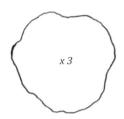

x 3

Template to trace

The stems, leaves and spent roses

Use green 2mm ribbon; make the stems in back stitch, 4mm (⅛") long. Whip the stitches with green 4mm ribbon. Use the same ribbon and ribbon stitch to make green sepals on the roses.

Make the leaves with green 7mm ribbon and green thread. Use ribbon stitch; read more *about ribbon stitch* on page 19 and *securing, shaping stitches* on page 20. Change to grey thread; make the veins in straight stitch.

Make sepals of the spent roses with green 4mm ribbon and ribbon stitch. Secure with green thread and tiny stab stitches. Make the thorns in straight stitch. Use green 4mm ribbon and twisted straight stitch to form the stem of the spent rose. Change to yellow 4mm ribbon; make a few tiny buds between the leaves in detached chain stitch.

Change to 45 thread; make yellow stamens with pistil stitch, wrapping thread three times around needle. Add brown stamens, using 311 thread and French knots, wrapping thread twice around the needle.

The roses

Use the blue pen; trace three circles from the template provided on the previous page. Cut out the shapes, place in water to dissolve the blue marks and place on towel to dry. Use the 45 thread; make a knot at the long end. Form a circle of running stitches along the edge.

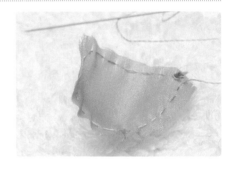

Make a soft ball from the yellow fibre about 1cm (⅜") in diameter; place it inside the circle. Pull the thread to gather ribbon around the ball. Use tiny stab stitches along the base of the ball to secure the gathered thread.

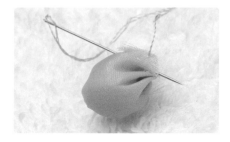

Place the ball on the design; secure in place along the base with stab stitches. Take needle to the back, come up through the centre of the ball. Make loose French knots to form the stamens, wrapping thread three times around the needle. Stitch through all the layers.

Change to the 311 thread; add a few brown stamens in between. Use loose French knots for a feathery texture. To make a loose French knot: wrap the thread lightly around the needle and use a gentle tension when you take needle to the back of your work. Change to green thread; make green disk in the very centre with the same stitch.

There are three shades of 13mm yellow ribbon to use for the rose petals. Alternate between 99, 53 and 56 for a lovely, lifelike effect.

Read about *making holes in fabric* and about *working with two needles* on page 20. Make the bottom layer of petals in ribbon stitch, working from the centre outwards. Work over the large tapestry needle to form raised petals. Use 91 thread and stab stitch to secure the petals on the base and the tip. This way, they won't pull out of shape in the next step. Make three to four petals for each rose.

Cut a 6cm (2⅜") length of 13mm ribbon (use any of the yellow shades) and thread up on a 16 chenille needle. Insert needle from top of your work, inserting it close to the centre of the rose and working between the ribbon stitches. Pull gently so that most of the ribbon remains on top of your work.

Apply glue to the ribbon and use the 18 tapestry needle to roll the ribbon. Use your fingers to press the edge of the ribbon against the needle and roll until the petal is short enough for the rose. See how the petal curls towards the yellow ball?

Remove needle at the back; leave a tail and secure it with 91 thread. Bring needle and thread to the top of your work, close to centre of rose. Secure base of petal with tiny stab stitches. Trim ribbon to remove frayed ends. Make five or six petals in the same way, allowing some petals to overlap the others.

Do this for three petals, curling and shaping them over the yellow ball. Curl until they overlap the centre. Remember to wipe your needle and hands before curling the next petal. Lift and support the petal against the ball with your fingertip. Use stab stitches to secure; insert needle into the base of the ball.

Roll the other petals, but this time curl them the other way – towards the fabric of the design. Shape and lift petals to form a pleasing shape. Use tiny stab stitch to secure in place.

Blue bow and Purple Emperors

You will need

RIBBON

Di van Niekerk's silk and organza ribbons

 25mm organza colour 89

7mm colour 64

THREAD

Use one strand of thread, unless suggested otherwise.

DMC six-strand embroidery floss

 809

Rajmahal Art.Silk

 129

226

NEEDLES

Embroidery size 9

Embroidery size 10

Tapestry size 18

OTHER

- Water-soluble fabric: 20cm (8") square (x 2)
- 15cm (6") hoop
- Black waterproof pigment ink pen. See page 23

STITCHES USED

Stitches are listed alphabetically in the stitch gallery on page 36.

Back stitch, blanket stitch, French knot, pistil stitch and straight/stab stitch.

Template to trace

Blue bow

Use the blue ribbon and make a bow. Stitch it onto your design with the blue thread, using tiny stab stitches.

Use tapestry needle; thread up with tail of the bow. Move needle through the loop of the bow. Twirl the ribbon to form a coiled tail; stitch in place with blue thread and tiny stab stitches. Cut off the excess ribbon and trim to remove the frayed ends.

Purple Emperor

Fill in the body with the 226 thread; make French knots close together. Change to 129 thread; make antennae in pistil stitch, wrapping thread twice around needle. Use straight stitch and add stripes over the knots to make shadows on the body.

Refer to chapter 8 pages 95 and 96: the wings are made the same way. Use blue organza ribbon and place in hoop as shown. Trace wings from the template on the previous page. Use 129 thread; fill in veins with back stitch and use blanket stitch for wing tips. Cut out and place in a bowl of water, as shown.

Pat dry and whilst still damp, secure wings onto design with 129 thread and tiny stab stitches – the same way as shown on page 96.

Chapter 17

Madame Gregoire Staechelin and Pearl Spotted Emperor

Actual size of the roses

Madame Gregoire Staechelin

You will need

RIBBON

Di van Niekerk's silk ribbons

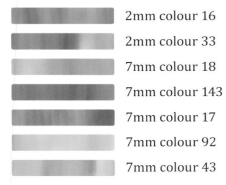

2mm colour 16

2mm colour 33

7mm colour 18

7mm colour 143

7mm colour 17

7mm colour 92

7mm colour 43

THREAD

Use one strand of thread, unless suggested otherwise.

DMC six-strand embroidery floss

523

Rajmahal Art.Silk

742

311

45

NEEDLES

Chenille size 16

Chenille size 18

Embroidery size 9

Embroidery size 10

Tapestry size 18

STITCHES USED

Stitches are listed alphabetically in the stitch gallery on page 36.

> Note: Read more about ribbon stitch on pages 19-20.

Back stitch, French knot, loop stitch, pistil stitch, ribbon stitch, running stitch, straight/stab stitch and whipped back stitch.

The stems, leaves and spent roses

Use brown thread and make thin stems in back stitch 3mm (⅛") in length. Whip stitches by inserting needle under and over every stitch two or three times. For thick green stems: use two strands of green thread and back stitch. Whip the stitches; use 2mm ribbon no. 16 for some stems and no. 33 for others. Wrap each stitch once or twice.

Read more *about ribbon stitch* on page 19 and make leaves in ribbon stitch. Alternate between shades for an interesting effect: use 7mm ribbon no. 143 for dark leaves, no. 17 for pale green leaves and no. 18 for brown-green leaves. Form the veins with brown thread and straight or back stitch.

Use yellow thread and pistil stitch to form the stamens, working from end of the stem outwards, wrapping thread twice around needle. Change to brown thread; make French knots between the yellow stamens, wrapping thread twice around needle. Use 2mm ribbon no. 33; make the green sepals in ribbon stitch, working over a tapestry needle to form looped stitches.

The roses

Use the no. 43 silk ribbon; form centre of each rose with three loop stitches, working over a tapestry needle. Secure loops with pink thread and tiny stab stitches. Read about *working with two needles* on page 20.

Change to the no. 92 ribbon and come up alongside the loops. Make small running stitches on the edge, spacing them about 2mm (¹⁄₁₆") apart. Stitch for about 2.5cm (1") or so.

Insert the chenille needle into the edge of the ribbon and gently pull the ribbon to the back. Come up alongside the ribbon and gently pull the thread to gather the ribbon slightly; take the thread to the back and come up alongside the ribbon.

Gather again, and this time insert the embroidery needle to the back, leaving the ribbon on the top of your work. Pull the thread softly to gather slightly and come up alongside the ribbon again.

Make a few stab stitches along the gathered edge to tuck the ribbon around the loops.

Take the ribbon to the back, leaving thread on top of your work.

Make ribbon stitches working with a gentle tension to form a looped petal. Secure it with tiny stab stitches at the base and tip and end off at the back.

Hint: For a larger rose, make more ribbon stitches, working around the rose with a gentle tension for a looped effect.

Use pink thread; secure and shape the petals with tiny stab stitches along edge and the base.

For open roses, gather ribbon but don't take it to the back until you reach the starting point again. Just the thread is taken to the back, once or twice, after gathering the ribbon. For upright petals, gather less and for flat petals, gather more. For an interesting effect, twirl the ribbon twice around the loops, making a second circle of petals.

Use yellow thread and pistil stitch to form the stamens, working from the centre outwards, wrapping thread twice around needle. The stamens will flatten the centre with lifelike results. Add a green French knot in the very centre to form the green disk, wrapping thread twice around the needle.

Thread up with 7mm no. 92 or 43; form the buds with a twirled ribbon rose. See page 33 for the technique. For a smaller bud, use a ribbon stitch. With 7mm ribbon no. 17 or 18, make the green calyx using same technique as shown for the red bud in chapter 12 on pages 122 and 123.

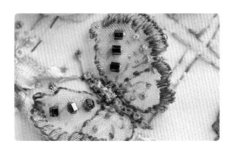

The Pearl Spotted Emperor is made in the same way as shown in chapter 8 on page 95.